# DOING BUSINESS IN POLAND

The Confederation of British Industry (CBI) is the voice of British business and is committed to alerting British companies to the commercial potential of Central and Eastern Europe. Its Initiative Central and Eastern Europe provides pragmatic and detailed advice on how to develop business and operate successfully in these emerging market economies.

The CBI also organises trade missions to the countries in the region and provides a forum in which to meet senior policy makers and business executives. Further details of all the CBI's Central and Eastern European activities are available from its headquarters.

CBI
Centre Point
103 New Oxford Street
London WC1A 1DU
Tel: 071-379-7400

# DOING BUSINESS IN POLAND

## SECOND EDITION

BMF • DELOITTE & TOUCHE, POLAND • NABARRO NATHANSON • RZB
SAATCHI & SAATCHI • GERALD EVE INTERNATIONAL • GJW • CTAD
BRITISH CHAMBER OF COMMERCE IN POLAND

This book is written on the basis of information constant in July 1994.

First published in 1991
Reprinted in 1992
Second edition 1994

Apart from any fair dealing for the purposes of research or private study, or criticism or review, as permitted under the Copyright, Designs and Patents Act, 1988, this publication may only be reproduced, stored or transmitted, in any form or by any means, with the prior permission in writing of the publishers, or in the case of reprographic reproduction in accordance with the terms of licences issued by the Copyright Licensing Agency. Enquiries concerning reproduction outside those terms should be sent to the publishers at the undermentioned address:

Kogan Page Limited
120 Pentonville Road
London N1 9JN

© Confederation of British Industry, 1991, 1994

**British Library Cataloguing in Publication Data**

A CIP record for this book is available from the British Library.

ISBN 0 7494 1473 1

Typeset by DP Photosetting, Aylesbury, Bucks
Printed in England by Clays Ltd, St Ives plc

# Contents

The Contributors  9

Foreword  13
*Waldemar Pawlak, Prime Minister of Poland*

Preface  15
*Alan J Lewis, CBE, Chairman, CBI Inititiative Central and Eastern Europe*

## PART I: THE BUSINESS CONTEXT  17

1. Poland and its Potential  19
   *BMF International Ltd*

2. Economic Reform  25
   *RZB-Austria*

3. Political Transformation  29
   *GJW Government Relations*

4. A New Legal Framework  33
   *Nabarro Nathanson*

5. Polish Business Culture  39
   *BMF International Ltd*

6. Market Intelligence  43
   *BMF International Ltd*

## PART II: THE BUSINESS INFRASTRUCTURE  47

7. Foreign Exchange  49
   *RZB-Austria*

8. Banking  53
   *RZB-Austria*

9. Privatisation  57
   *BMF International Ltd*

10. Restructuring State Enterprises  63
    *BMF International Ltd*

11. Foreign Investment  71
    *Nabarro Nathanson*

12. Capital Markets  77
    *BMF International Ltd*

13. Valuation and Accounting  83
    *Deloitte & Touche, Warsaw*

14. The Fiscal Regime  89
    *Deloitte & Touche, Warsaw*

15. Property  95
    *Gerald Eve International*

16. Employment Law  105
    *Nabarro Nathanson*

17. The Labour Market  113
    *Jakubowski CTAD Ltd*

18. The Environment  117
    *BMF International Ltd*

19. Utilities  123
    *British Chamber of Commerce in Poland*

## PART III: THE OPTIONS FOR WESTERN BUSINESS  127

20. Export and Import  129
    *Deloitte & Touche, Warsaw*

21. Agencies, Distributorships and Franchises  133
    *Nabarro Nathanson*

22. Marketing  137
    *Saatchi & Saatchi Advertising Poland*

23. Trade Finance  147
    *RZB-Austria*

24. Intellectual Property   151
    *Nabarro Nathanson*

25. Project Finance   159
    *RZB-Austria*

26. Investment Strategy   163
    *BMF International Ltd*

27. Investment Finance   169
    *RZB-Austria*

28. Setting Up a Company   173
    *Nabarro Nathanson*

## PART IV: CASE STUDIES                                              177

1. Elektrim   179
2. Pilkington   183
3. Cadbury Schweppes   187
4. Unicorn Poland   191

## APPENDICES                                                          195

1. Opportunities by Sector   197
   *BMF International Ltd*
2. Economic Assistance   215
3. Sources of Further Information   223

*Index   231*

# The Contributors

**BMF International** are part of the BMF Group who are one of the leading companies in Poland committed to adding value to Polish industry through financial and operational restructuring, and the introduction of Western business practices. Current activities include the provision of high quality corporate finance, management consulting, government advisory and asset management services. The BMF Group operates out of Warsaw, Katowice and London and works in close association with Swiss Bank Corporation.

**Deloitte & Touche Poland** was established in Warsaw in November 1990, and is part of Deloitte Touche Tohmatsu International, one of the world's largest accounting, auditing, tax and management consultancy firms. The company has now grown to over 120 people, and operates in Gdańsk and Kraków as well as in Warsaw. The firm has considerable experience in assisting Western companies in entering the Polish market, and advises a large number of multinational clients as well as some significant Polish-owned enterprises. It has also acted as advisor to the Polish government on privatisations and the restructuring of state-owned enterprises.

**Nabarro Nathanson** opened its Warsaw office in 1991 and has established itself as a prominent Polish and international law firm. Most of its lawyers are Polish and the firm advises on the laws of Poland, the UK, the USA and Germany, as well as international law. The firm also advises on a broad variety of commercial matters representing both Polish and foreign clients. Nabarro Nathanson has advised on many start-up operations, handling the negotiation and preparation, in English and Polish, of joint venture agreements, management agreements, licence agreements and other commercial documentation. Nabarro Nathanson has a specialist real estate department in Warsaw. It also advises on banking and finance matters; all forms of equity and loan transactions; energy projects and on acquisitions and privatisations, including the Mass Privatisation Programme. Nabarro Nathanson is fully versed in the many issues, such as tax, employment, real estate acquisition, intellectual property and environmental law, that face companies operating in Poland.

**The Austrian Raiffeisen Banking Group** operates on a local level throughout Austria with 733 Raiffeisen banks having 1724 branches acting as universal banks offering a full range of banking services. The 'Raiffeisen-Landeszentralen' operate on a regional level for the federal provinces and are, simultaneously, shareholders of the Raiffeisen Zentralbank Oesterreich AG (RZB-Austria). The activities of RZB-Austria comprise both its own commercial business and its role as the central institution for the Raiffeisen Banking Group overall. RZB-Austria has an extensive commitment in Central and Eastern Europe with majority holdings in Raiffeisen-Centrobank SA in Warsaw, Unicbank Rt in Budapest, Raiffeisenbank in the Czech Republic and Tatra Banka in Slovakia. RZB-Austria is also represented in Moscow, Kiev and Sofia. In addition, Raiffeisen Investment AG, Raiffeisen Ost Invest and Raiffeisen Property Invest, which are RZB-Austria subsidiaries located in Vienna, are involved in consulting, equity investment and real estate development in this region.

**Saatchi & Saatchi Advertising Worldwide** is one of the world's leading advertising and communications networks with 143 offices in 77 countries. Saatchi & Saatchi Advertising established its first office in eastern/central Europe in Budapest in April 1990, closely followed by Warsaw and Prague. Today, they have the leading advertising agency network in the region with offices in Bucharest, Sofia, Ljubljana, Moscow, St Petersburg, Zagreb and Tallinn. Representation is planned in 1994 in Tirana and Skopje.

**Gerald Eve International** (Poland) is the Polish subsidiary of Gerald Eve, one of the UK's leading firms of chartered surveyors. It was set up following the political changes that took place in Central and Eastern Europe in the late 1980s, and offers agency, real estate consultancy and financing services to clients operating in the Polish market. The company is now the market leader in Poland for the provision of real estate agency and consultancy advice. To support the wide range of services offered to clients, the firm has a multidisciplinary staff comprising professionals with qualifications in property, business consultancy, finance, economics, law and architecture.

**GJW Government Relations** is the specialist political consultancy and lobbying firm providing a comprehensive service on all matters relating to government and political relations across the whole of Central and Eastern Europe and Russia. Its office in Warsaw, opened in 1991, provides a full range of professional services to international as well as Polish clients. GJW also has offices in Budapest, Prague, Bucharest, Sofia and Moscow, in addition to London and Brussels.

**Jakubowski CTAD Ltd** was formed in 1992 as an associate company of Cambridge Training and Development Ltd to channel its expertise on the emerging needs for consultancy and project management in Poland. The company is unique in that it uses a task force of British-born Polish-speaking professionals for project work in Poland. Services include problem-solving and troubleshooting, project management, organisational practice, business development, privatisation, market research and training and learning systems.

**The British Chamber of Commerce in Poland** is an organisation which aims to service the needs of the British business community in Poland and Polish companies with British interests. Membership is currently in excess of 160. Events include monthly breakfast meetings, conferences and seminars. Subcommittees monitor different market sectors and there is a regular newsletter.

# Foreword

Poland was the first country to break free of the former Soviet bloc and from the command economy. Poland today is the first Central Eastern European economy to show strong growth – the fastest in Europe – after emerging from deep recession following economic restructuring. Gross national product (GNP) has been growing for two years; in 1994 industrial output has increased by nearly 10 per cent compared to the same period a year ago. The private sector is developing rapidly; today it employs around 60 per cent of the nation's workforce. Despite such negative phenomena as unemployment or the impoverishment of certain social groups, Poland deserves to be perceived as a country with great possibilities and perspectives for development.

The government's recently published socio-economic development programme 'A Strategy for Poland' foresees that in the years 1994–97, GNP will rise by 22 per cent, exports by 34 per cent and inflation will fall to below 10 per cent. Despite our obligation to control unemployment and its attendant social problems we nevertheless intend to maintain financial and budgetary discipline, so as not to allow a resurgence of inflation and, above all, to create conditions for economic activity in Poland.

We want those conditions to be stable, so that Polish and foreign enterprises can plan ahead with a good measure of certainty.

Our economic development programme makes the assumption that exports and direct foreign capital investment will act as the main driving forces for growth. We are committed to continuing a policy of opening our doors to global trade and investment; the association agreement concluded between the European Union (EU) and Poland foresees the creation of a free trade zone for industrial products by the year 2000.

Our ultimate goal is full EU membership, with Poland integrating itself into the very bloodstream of Europe's economy. With this aim in mind, we are creating within our economy a comparable business environment, harmonising with Europe on issues like competition law, intellectual property rights and other such aspects.

Poland, as a signatory of the Uruguay Round Final Act, will soon become a member of the newly created World Trade Organisation. We have also started negotiating for Poland's rapid entry into the Organisation for Economic Co-operation and Development (OECD).

For those who wish to do business with us, these are signals that we fully intend to comply with the accepted rules of trade, commerce and investment.

Foreign investors have come to understand the attractions of the Polish market – its size, its highly qualified workforce, its perspectives for development its central location in Europe and the long experience of Polish firms in trade and co-operation with Eastern Europe.

Poland has neither border disputes nor ethnic unrest; we have no territorial demands on other countries, nor do other countries have territorial demands on Poland. These are factors that companies making long-term appraisals for investment decisions cannot ignore.

Despite the intense global competition for inward investment, I am personally convinced that Poland – placed as it is on the crossroads of Europe's east–west and north–south trade routes – has much to offer. For its part, my government will do all it can to ensure that Polish and foreign investors benefit from the profits flowing from their economic activity in our country.

*Waldemar Pawlak*
*Prime Minister of the Republic of Poland*

# Preface

Poland is establishing itself as one of Europe's most dynamic and exciting markets with growth rates more usually associated with south-east Asia. While four years of far-reaching economic reform have inevitably caused dislocation and hardship, Poland is now reaping the benefits of taking the fast road in adjusting to free market norms. Not all the elements of a deregulated, open economy may be in place, but prospects for developing business appear to be increasingly positive.

This is the second edition of a book originally published in 1991. Much has happened since then, as free market policies have been introduced and a wealth of operating experience has been accumulated. This new edition is designed to give international companies a breakdown of the potential Poland offers, as well as providing a commentary on the market's political and economic context, along with practical guidance on how to go about developing business.

The CBI is grateful to the principal contributors: BMF, a leading business advisor and one of the pioneers of venture capital in Poland; RZB, a leading Austrian bank firmly established in Poland; Deloitte & Touche, a major accountancy practice with a significant local presence; and Nabarro Nathanson, a leading international legal firm, who have run an office in Poland since the earliest days of market reform.

Supporting chapters have been contributed by: the local office of Saatchi & Saatchi on marketing; Michael Roskelly of Gerald Eve International in Warsaw on Poland's fast developing property markets; by CTAD Jakubowski on the labour market; by GJW Government Relations on Poland's political outlook; and by the British Chamber of Commerce on the quality of support services that international companies can expect to find.

The CBI is grateful as well to the European Bank for Reconstruction and Development, the World Bank, the EC's PHARE programme and the UK's Know How Fund for the information they have all supplied. Michael Dembinski, Jagoda Bok, Jane Belova and Robert Howell have also made valuable contributions.

Four case studies in Part IV cover different corporate responses to new market conditions. Elektrim is a major Polish corporate that has restructured itself to become one of the most attractive stocks listed on the Warsaw Exchange. Pilkington is running a £100m project to set up Poland's first float glass plant and Cadbury Schweppes has commissioned a new £20m confectionery factory. Finally, Unicorn, an Anglo-Polish start-up in 1990, has now built itself into a leading light in Polish software. The CBI is grateful to these companies, who have been prepared to express their experiences so freely.

This book forms part of a wider, ongoing campaign to keep our members alive to the potential Poland offers. These efforts have been immeasurably strengthened by our close working relations with the Department of Trade and Industry in London and the commercial office of the British embassy in Warsaw. Over the past year, it has been particularly encouraging to see the impact John Evans, the UK's export promoter for Poland, has been making.

The CBI thanks all those whose time and effort have made this book possible. I hope it will provide international companies with the guidance and information they need to develop and grow in Poland. There is an extensive list of contacts at the end of the book for those with questions still to ask.

*Alan J Lewis CBE*
*Chairman, CBI Initiative Central and Eastern Europe*
*September 1994*

*Part I*

# The Business Context

# 1

# Poland and its Potential

## BMF International Ltd

## INTRODUCTION

In terms of land mass, Poland is the largest country in Central Europe, occupying an area as large as the Czech Republic, Slovakia and Hungary combined. Poland also has an ethnically homogeneous, Catholic and highly educated population of 38.6 million, which is the largest of the former Comecon countries. The country is strategically located between the former USSR and Western Europe, and on the north–south axis between the Scandinavian countries and Central Eastern Europe. Poland is already making moves to form closer links with the EU and with the country's strong historical ties with the Commonwealth of Independent States (CIS) there is a huge opportunity for Poland to benefit from growth in both the East and the West.

## HISTORY

Modern Polish history starts around the ninth century when the country began gradually to form its own identity. By the fourteenth century, Poland had become a European superpower, stretching from the Baltic States to Hungary and all the way east past Kiev. Unfortunately, due to Poland's geographic location, the country was subject to many successive invasions which finally led to its partitioning in 1795 by Russia, Prussia and Austria. There followed 150 years of suppression, which culminated in several uprisings as the Poles fought to keep their own identity and re-establish their country. It was not until 1918 that Poland finally managed to reclaim its sovereignty. As a victim of repression, therefore, Poland had become a symbol of resistance.

The onset of the Second World War brought terrible devastation to the country with an estimated 20 per cent of the population perishing. The end of the war saw Poland firmly behind the Iron Curtain and the introduction of a Communist regime. Despite wide-scale nationalisation, however, Polish communism in comparison to elsewhere in Eastern Europe was relatively mild. The general population always kept a cynical and suspicious attitude towards their Communist leaders, and this led to public demonstrations in 1956, 1968 and 1970. In 1980 there was the rise of the Solidarity movement which united workers with intellectual dissidents, again demonstrating the lack of public support for the government. In December 1981, however, the dissidents were pushed underground as martial law was imposed in order to pre-empt Russian intervention. By 1989 the combination of a swell in popular dissatisfaction with the government, miserable economic conditions and the onset of *perestroika* in Russia led to the bloodless fall of Communism in Poland. The first free elections since the war were held in 1989 and the new reformist Mazowiecki government began the establishment of a free market economy.

## THE ESTABLISHMENT OF A FREE MARKET ECONOMY

Since 1989 the economy has been undergoing profound changes. Under Finance Minister Balcerowicz the Poles chose to instigate shock therapy reforms, which included liberalising prices, slashing state subsidies and making the zloty internally convertible. These policies, whose main function was to introduce a market economy, took the country into deep recession as industrial output fell in 1990/1 by over 30 per cent and inflation soared to over 500 per cent. As the first Comecon country to embark upon these market reforms, however, Poland has been steadily recovering from recession and in 1993 the economy grew by 4 per cent. Poland is now one of the fastest growing countries in Europe. Finance Minister Kolodko has reiterated the government's commitment to growth in Poland by announcing his 'Strategy for Poland' in which the government intends to increase gross domestic product (GDP) by 22 per cent over the next four years. At the same time the government is committed to bringing inflation down below 10 per cent, increasing real wages by 10 per cent, increasing private consumption by well over 10 per cent and reducing unemployment to below 14 per cent.

The driving force in this turn around has been the increase in consumer demand and the dramatic rise in private sector activity. The private sector now accounts for over 50 per cent of GDP, having risen from 29 per cent in 1989. This private sector development has occurred not through government-led mass privatisation (the government has been cautious in introducing the 'Mass Privatisation Programme', although this is now due to be started by the end of 1994), but rather through organic growth. Future growth in Poland is going to come largely from increased trade both with the West and East. Unfortunately the restructuring of the Polish economy coincided with the collapse of the former Comecon export markets and a

## CENTERTEL RENT-A-PHONE

From Warsaw to Cracow, Gdańsk to Poznań, (and anywhere in between) the freedom to communicate is a noble ideal. Centertel, Poland's only cellular phone network, has made that ideal a reality. With our state-of-the-art mobile telephones, Centertel is all the support you need to keep in contact while on the move in Poland. As our network covers all major transport routes and urban centres, you need never worry about accessibility.

For more information call:

**0-90 234567**

deep recession in Western Europe. In response Poland has shown a dramatic structural change in its foreign trade, with Germany now being the key trading partner – accounting for about one-third of total trade. The Comecon countries, which in 1985 accounted for 51 per cent of total trade, was less than 25 per cent in 1993. EU exports, on the other hand, which in 1989 accounted for only 28 per cent, by 1993 had risen to 75 per cent.

In the long term Poland's commitment to join the EU should bring about not only increased trade but also greater flows of capital into the country. At present Poland has an associated agreement with the EU which is aimed at gradually liberalising trade and providing assistance in areas as diverse as the environment, drug control and monetary policy. At the end of 1993 CEFTA (Central European Free Trade Agreement) was established with the objective of creating a free trade area for most trade products within Central Europe by 2001.

One of the main barriers to growth in Poland has been the huge amount of foreign debt that the country accumulated during the 1970s and 1980s. This stood at US$48 billion in 1990 or 80 per cent of GDP. Fortunately, however, in March 1994 Poland signed a debt reduction agreement with the London Club of commercial creditors, cutting the aggregate Polish obligations of US$13.2 billion by more than 40 per cent. Only weeks later, the final tranche of a 50 per cent reduction of Polish debt (some US$33 billion) *viv-à-vis* the Paris Club of public creditors was also approved.

This outstanding debt issue has kept many foreign investors out of Poland. Inward investment into the country has only been a fraction of that going into Hungary or the Czech Republic, even in absolute terms, let alone GDP per capita.

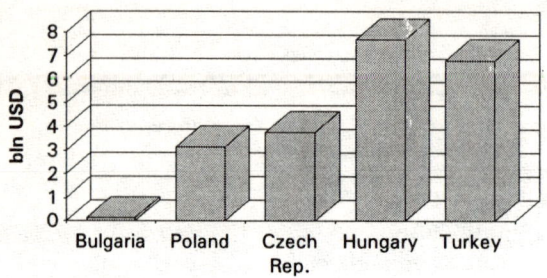

Figure 1.1 *Foreign investments 1990–1993*

Source: OECD Databank

With the resolution of the recent debt negotiations foreign investment is expected to increase substantially. The largest foreign investor in Poland to date is Fiat who have committed US$1.7 billion in a joint venture with FSO, a local car manufacturer. Other major investors include such companies as Pepsico, Procter and Gamble, International Paper, ABB, Thompson, Unilever, Lucchini Group, France Telecom and Pilkington.

## OPPORTUNITIES FOR THE FOREIGN INVESTOR

Poland has a well-diversified economy with an extensive manufacturing sector and a large service sector. The industrial sector is the largest in the economy, accounting for nearly half of GDP and employing 29 per cent of the labour force.

**Table 1.1** *Breakdown of GDP structure*

|  | 1989 | 1992 |
|---|---|---|
| **TOTAL** | 100.0 | 100.0 |
| Industry | 44.1 | 38.0 |
| Construction | 8.2 | 8.6 |
| Agriculture | 11.8 | 6.8 |
| Forestry | 1.1 | 0.6 |
| Transport | 3.9 | 3.9 |
| Telecommunication | 0.6 | 1.8 |
| Trade | 16.3 | 14.4 |
| Other | 14.0 | 25.9 |

Source: The 1993 Polish Main Statistical Yearbook

In terms of GDP Poland is classified as a middle-income country with a per capita income of less than US$2000. This is significantly less than that of Western neighbours and even former Comecon counterparts. This gap in GDP per capita gives Poland the opportunity to catch up with her neighbours on standards of living rise.

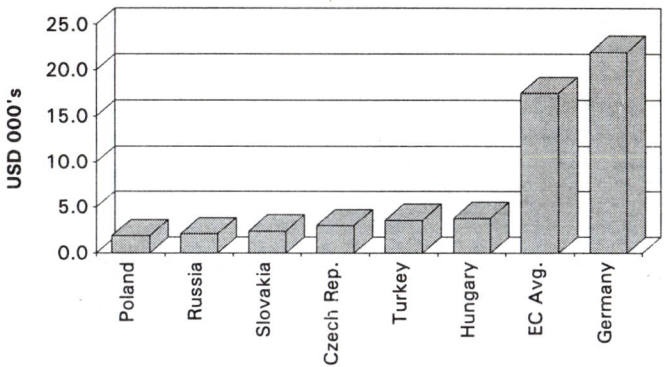

Figure 1.2 *1992 GDP per capita*
Source: *The Economist World Book, 1994*

There are also country advantages upon which a competitive edge and success can be built. The level of technical skills in Polish manufacturing is generally on a par with West European standards and provides an excellent basis for attracting Western partners. This makes Poland an ideal strategic manufacturing base together with its crossroads geographical location – wage costs of a fraction of those in the West.

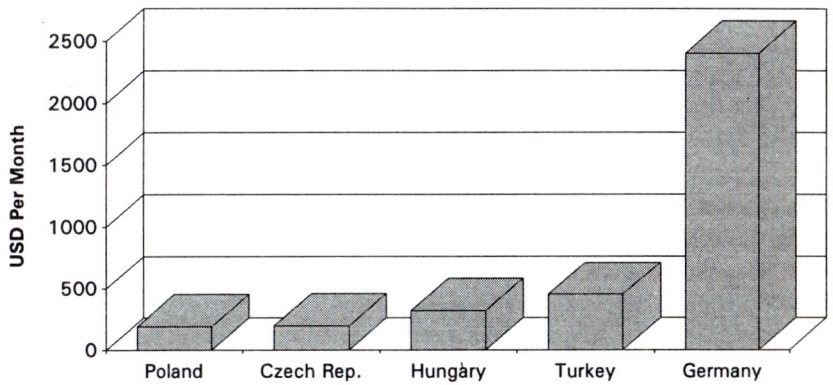

Figure 1.3 *Low wage rates*
Source: *Business Central Europe, October 1993*

New economic institutions have developed both inside and outside government. New commercial banks, private insurance companies and other financial intermediaries have become actors in the economy, and private enterprises have expanded in number, size and the range of their activities.

Market-oriented instruments for managing the economy have also been created. Prices are now the fundamental economic regulators, a modern tax system is being put in place, budget processes have been made more transparent and instruments for indirect control over the money supply have been introduced.

On top of Poland's advantages as an industrial location there are also values that are difficult to quantify, though very important for a country's position in international competition. Among Poles there is a deep appreciation for hard work and economic success. A major contribution to such an attitude and support stems from the large number of well-educated and skilled Polish expatriates for whom the changes in their native country have suddenly opened unexpected opportunities. With a significant number of these expatriates now returning and with the country's historical bias towards Western cultural roots, Poland's road to a full membership in the EU and to the Western community may be smoother than many expect.

Although many foreign investors have been wary of the political situation in Poland which has hitherto been somewhat fractious, all parties have demonstrated their commitment to the economic reforms. This has been amply demonstrated by the re-election of the Socialists in September 1993 who have made no policy changes in the reforms. The political environment, therefore, is favourable for increasing further foreign investment.

Finally, perhaps the most compelling reason to invest in Poland is the quality of the workforce who have adequately demonstrated that they have the entrepreneurialism, dynamism and resourcefulness to take Poland full speed into the twenty-first century.

# 2

# Economic Reform
## RZB-Austria

### THE PROGRESS OF ECONOMIC REFORM

Following the significant economic changes initiated by the first Solidarity government in 1990, the process of economic reform has proceeded in Poland. Indeed reform has developed a life of its own, insofar as the forces of entrepreneurship unleashed by removal of previous restrictions have led to the private sector playing an ever more significant part in the national economy (it currently accounts for 60 per cent). The Polish economy has clearly been the most successful amongst the former Comecon countries. Not only was it the first of these countries to emerge from recession, seeing positive GDP growth in 1992, but also, in 1993, its GDP growth of 4 per cent was the fastest in Europe. This figure is expected to be at least as high in 1994.

The main impetus for Poland's strong economic performance appears to be domestic investment and consumption, rather than government spending or net exports. While the role of consumption may appear paradoxical in view of tight monetary and income controls (real wages fell by nearly 3 per cent in 1993), nevertheless retail sales increased by 11 per cent over the same period. The explanation from this would appear to lie in an increase in incomes from self-employment, while activity in the grey economy is probably a major factor.

Most subsidies and market distortions have been removed in Poland. The introduction in July 1993 of value added tax (VAT) (set at 22 per cent), together with rising tax receipts as a result of economic growth, will swell government coffers at a time it is under pressure to increase social expenditure. On the industrial front, many of the most energy intensive and polluting plants have been either closed, restructured or reduced in scale and this process is likely to accelerate as other, more dynamic areas of the economy are able to expand sufficiently to absorb the surplus labour.

Privatisation, which will continue to play a major role in the ongoing transformation of the Polish economy, by decentralising decision making and thus increasing the response to market signals, has been slower than might have been expected. Nevertheless, of a total of approximately 10,000 state-owned enterprises, 28 per cent had been privatised by the end of 1993. Moreover, the tempo of privatisation is expected to receive a major shot in the arm with the implementation of the long-heralded Mass Privatisation Programme confidently expected in the second half of 1994.

Domestic inflation has continued to fall since the dramatic liberalisation of prices in 1990 (which led to annual inflation topping 585 per cent) and in 1993 it amounted to 35 per cent. This figure was adversely affected by several official price increases (eg fuel, transport, telecommunications) and by the introduction of VAT. Inflation is in any event expected to fall to 25–27 per cent in 1994 and to 21 per cent in 1995. The National Bank of Poland has set itself the primary target of controlling inflation and is thus likely to keep tight hold over domestic interest rates. Nevertheless, in order to keep exports competitive, the National Bank has adopted a policy of crawling peg devaluation of 1.5 per cent per month against a basket of currencies. In addition, there have been a number of more substantial devaluations, in May 1991, February 1992 and in August 1993. As at the end of 1993 the exchange rate was Zl21,300 to the US dollar.

The International Monetary Fund (IMF) continues to provide backing to Poland in its economic reforms and approved the passing of another tight budget for 1994, which will maintain the budget below 5 per cent of GDP. This step facilitated the agreement in March 1993 with the London Club of commercial bank creditors concerning the reduction and restructuring of Poland's US$13.2 billion of commercial debt. The agreement has also paved the way for the second and final stage of a 50 per cent cut in Poland's US$33 billion debt to the Paris Club of official government creditors, which was agreed in April 1991. Taken together, the Paris and London Club agreements should open up the prospect of the medium and long-term capital being attracted to Poland which is required to finance the development of infrastructure, as the essential element for sustainable economic growth.

Poland's balance of payments has deteriorated over the last two years, reaching an estimated US$2 billion at the end of 1993. This need not, however, be taken as an entirely negative signal, on account of the high demands of a rapidly growing economy and available statistics suggest that capital goods are the main source of the deficit. Moreover, the recession in Poland's major trading partners in the EC (notably Germany) is undoubtedly depressing the level of exports, as are EC restrictions on imports from Poland and other Central European countries.

Rising unemployment has been an unpleasant side-effect of economic reform. Before 1989 the only unemployment was of the hidden variety, with factories hoarding labour to meet unexpected contingencies. By the end of 1990, however, unemployment amounted to over 1.1 million or 6.3 per cent of the economically active population. This figure has risen steadily since, amounting to 2.1 million at the end of 1991, 2.5 million at the end of 1992 and 2.9 million (15.7 per cent) by the end of 1993, although the rate of increase has slowed down.

Among the employed workforce there has been a marked shift, in percentage terms, from the public to the private sector. In part this has been due to the dynamic growth of new private businesses, as well as to privatisation, but also to the decline of the state sector. It is interesting to note, for example, that of those who had worked previously and were seeking work at the end of 1993, 58 per cent had previously worked in the state sector, as against 42 per cent in the private sector. The highest increases in unemployment in the final quarter of 1993 were reported in state administrative and local authority positions.

The Warsaw Stock Exchange was reopened on 16 April 1991, 52 years after its closure in 1939. The newly revived market got off to a quiet start, with trade in just five newly privatised companies being undertaken by seven stockbroking firms.

In 1993 the Warsaw Stock Exchange really came into its own. The WIG index rose more than 11-fold in local currency terms (and by over 700 per cent in US dollar terms), ending the year at a level of 12,439 points, thereby easily outperforming all other stock markets in the world. While the number of listed companies on the exchange only increased by six, most of these new issues were accompanied by ever rising public interest. Moreover, the market's capitalisation during the year increased more than tenfold to US$2.6 billion.

The main catalyst behind the dramatic events on the Warsaw Stock Exchange may be seen as the reduction in domestic interest rates in February 1993, which led to a reduction in the growth of bank deposits. Moreover, Poland's rapidly improving economic prospects, especially compared with the other new democracies in Central Europe, came increasingly to be recognised, particularly among foreign investors. This combination of domestic and international money served to drive the market up to regular new record levels. Few setbacks were suffered along the way, although the election of the reformed communist SLD in September 1993 did spark off a 30 per cent fall in prices. This period was not, however, sustained, as shrewd investors perceived the availability of bargains. At the same time, domestic investors were not slow to pick up the message given by sharply rising prices and indeed by the end of the year, with the market continuing to set new records at frequent intervals, it was domestic and not foreign investors who were providing the main boost to the market's liquidity.

While valuations may have run up too high in the course of 1993, making subsequent corrections inevitable, the success of the market is unlikely to disappear from the popular imagination. An investment culture appears to have been born in Poland.

# 3

# Political Transformation

## GJW Government Relations

On 4 June 1989, as a result of 'round table' negotiations, Poland held its first post-war parliamentary elections and out of the 460 seats in the Sejm (the lower house of the Parliament), 160 were allocated to the opposition Solidarity camp.

In July 1989, the newly formed Parliament elected Wojciech Jaruzelski, former prime minister and the first secretary of the Polish United Labour Party (PZPR) as president. He was the only candidate and was elected with a majority of just one vote. After General Kiszczak, the initiator of the 'round table' talks and the internal affairs minister, failed to set up a government, the Sejm charged Tadeusz Mazowiecki, a member of Solidarity camp, with this task.

## THE GREAT DIVIDE

In January 1990, bowing to heavy external and internal pressures, PZPR decided to dissolve itself and a new party, Socjaldemokracja Rzeczpospolitej Polskiej (SdRP) was immediately formed to fill the gap left by PZPR. SdRP was the successor to PZPR and took over all its property. This started the big social debate on the problems of clearing the accounts with the past. Whereas one part of Solidarity opted for closing the account, another faction believed that those who had been responsible for the crimes and atrocities committed under Communism should face prosecution. This dilemma, as well as the question of Lech Walesa's role on the political scene, split the Solidarity camp. The people in the pro-prosecution camp assembled around Jaroslaw Kaczynski, forming a new political party – Centre Alliance (PC).

A powerful political movement began to form around Prime Minister Tadeusz Mazowiecki, in opposition to Walesa, taking the name Democratic Union (UD).

The presidential campaign that began after Jaruzelski's resignation, served only to deepen the political divisions in society. In the end a majority (75 per cent) elected Lech Walesa in the second round vote.

Mazowiecki, who ran for the presidential post, resigned from his post as prime minister after losing the election and Jan Bielecki established a new government, gathering politicians around him in the newly formed Liberal-Democrats Congress (KLD).

All the party regroupings and reorganisation set the scene for the 1991 Sejm elections, contested under proportional representation. These elections were the first fully democratic elections held in Poland since the Second World War.

The new Sejm started its first session in November 1991. Jan Olszewski was elected to form a new government, which he achieved. However, his administration often frustrated Walesa. Walesa was anxious to press ahead with vital reforms, particularly in the area of the economy, but he found his efforts slowed or undone by the sluggishness and inefficiency of the government. This situation was resolved when the government was dismissed by a speeded-up procedure in the late hours of 1 June 1992. The reason given was the so-called 'Scrutiny Act', which was passed by the Sejm two weeks earlier. The Act provided some compromising information about many members of the government. This affair reopened the debate on political crimes of the past, and whether there was any merit to be gained by pursuing the issue further, especially as the courts had been shown to be impotent when the official dossiers were kept secret.

After the dismissal of the Olszewski government, Walesa appointed Waldemar Pawlak of the Polish Peasant Party (PSL) to set up a replacement government. Pawlak failed after 33 days of negotiations and Hanna Suchocka (Democratic Union) replaced him. Suchocka's new government incorporated members of six of the post-Solidarity parties, representing a wide spectrum of policies and programmes. Suchocka made continuation of the privatisation programme and reformation of the bureaucracy her top priorities.

## BACK TO POWER

Polish society had, in the years immediately following the fall of Communism, suffered the widespread effects common to a country in such a transitional stage of development – lowering of living standards, widening gaps between levels of income and rising unemployment due to the attempted transformation of the industrial sector. Despite government assurances that such symptoms were temporary, the people had seen their expectations following the transition from Communist rule dashed. People were also rather disillusioned with the instability of the political parties and the belief developed that all political affairs boiled down to 'fighting for the most lucrative posts'. This general lack of confidence in the government and the wider arena of politics led the president to dissolve the Sejm, with new elections held in September 1993. In these elections, the coalition of Democratic Left Alliance (SLD), post-Communism party and the Polish Peasant Party (PSL), won a majority of about 290 seats out of 460.

The new Sejm appointed Waldemar Pawlak as prime minister and he set up the government allocating posts between the main coalition parties. Control of the economic departments and the ministry of justice were given to Democratic Left Alliance (SLD). The ministries of education, ecology and agriculture went to PSL politicians. The president retained the more sensitive ministries, including interior affairs, defence and foreign affairs (this arrangement was guaranteed by the 'Small Constitution' – the series of amendments to the 1952 constitution). In addition to this, the new government has seen the introduction of a new upper-level staff, both in the voivodes and the central administration.

The opposition parties, wary of repeating the experiences of the elections, have reformed into various alliances or new parties. The Freedom Union (UW) was formed as an alliance of Democratic Union (UD) and Liberal-Democrats Congress (KLD). Several new groups were formed just ahead of the local elections on 19 July. There are two main alliances: Centre Alliance (PC) under Jaroslaw Kaczynski, Confederation for an Independent Poland (KPN) under Leszek Moczulski, the Union of Real Politics (UPR) under Janusz Korwin-Mikke; and Christian National Union (ZChN) under Wieslaw Chrzanowski, with small nationalist parties.

Recently the Sejm has passed the economic plan known as 'Strategy for Poland', proposed by Finance Minister Grzegorz Kolodko, which outlines the socio-economic policy for the years 1994–7. On the basis of the decree on the introduction and implementation of Strategy for Poland, ministers and heads of central administrative offices have prepared lists of ministerial tasks arising from the strategy, and the drafts of new legislative documents and indispensable changes to legislation are already in place. Also, the Public Procurement Law, which had been under consideration since 1992, was finally passed last May. At present there are some major pieces of legislation under consideration, including:

- the introduction of a so-called 'equalisation payment' tariff on foreign imports of foodstuffs, which are at least 10 per cent cheaper than Polish products;
- a bill to restrict the foreign capital share in the domestic media to a maximum of 30 per cent;
- a draft law on the ratification of the Concordat between Poland and the Holy See.

Local government elections on 19 June were Poland's first local elections since 1990. While left-wing parties run more independently, the right wing formed various coalitions. The average turnout was 34.2 per cent. The

Democratic Left Alliance (SLD) made most of the gains; it won in 75 out of 141 cities, where it had registered lists with their candidates for councillors.

The next major political event on Poland's political scene are the presidential elections in June 1995. Walesa, who has already confirmed that he will run for the presidency, is not the most popular candidate. According to the recent opinion polls, the leader of the Democratic Left Alliance (SLD), Aleksander Kwasniewski, would be the best candidate, followed by Prime Minister Pawlak and Foreign Minister Olechowski. President Walesa is in fourth place, together with former Foreign Minister Skubiszewski and the leader of the Non-party Bloc in Support of Reforms (BBWR), Zbigniew Religa.

# 4

# A New Legal Framework

*Nabarro Nathanson*

## INTRODUCTION

Since the changes which began in 1989, Poland has undoubtedly achieved a great deal in the area of legal reform. There have been new laws in the areas of privatisation, foreign investment, property law, exchange control, securities, tax, anti-monopoly, bankruptcy and banking.

In order to create the legal framework necessary for a free market economy, such laws had to be enacted in some cases without any precedent and in other cases by way of amendment to existing legislation. Poland has a legal tradition dating back to before the imposition of the Socialist system and the concepts of that pre-Socialist era were never completely suppressed. The law dealing with companies is a good example of this. The provisions in question were contained in the Commercial Code enacted in 1934 and although the Code itself was repealed the provisions on companies remained in force. This was necessary as a number of activities were carried out through state-owned corporate entities. Other laws in the commercial field existed before Socialism and remained in force, such as those on intellectual property, currently being updated.

The Civil Code was enacted in 1964 and was the first codification of civil law in Poland. Prior to the Second World War there had been a Code of Obligations (1933), but not a Civil Code. Before Poland regained its independence in 1918 the legal position had been complicated due to the different occupying powers. The laws of Austria, Prussia and Russia applied to the areas under their control and for a while in the nineteenth century the Napoleonic Code applied directly to the area known for a period as the Kingdom of Poland.

Hence, Poland has always been a civil law jurisdiction and the communist period never destroyed the core principles of this system.

## PROPERTY

An important task at the outset was to remove the concepts of the Socialist system from the Constitution of 1952. The Constitution contained provisions dealing with the Socialist classifications of property; these divided property into social property (state owned), personal property (such as one's house) and private property (some remaining individual ownership of economic activities, expected to 'wither away', which of course they never did). These classifications were removed by the amendments to the Constitution in 1989.

The Constitution now contains provisions for the protection of private property and Article 7 reads as follows: 'The Polish state protects and fully guarantees private property'. Once the concepts of Socialist property had been removed from the Constitution, it was necessary to make amendments to the Civil Code, and other legislation which contained further provisions dealing with the Socialist nature of property and the rights of the state. Important amendments were made to the Civil Code in 1989 and to the Land Use and Management Act in 1990. State Socialist property had been considered the highest form of property and endowed with 'indivisibility'. The special status of state property and its indivisibility was abolished. One of the results of this was that state enterprises became able to own, manage and dispose of their assets. In the case of land they were empowered to acquire long-term leases ('perpetual usufruct').

All property is now treated equally. However, property problems still remain with respect to questions of ownership and the claims of former owners. The question of reprivatisation is particularly complex and needs resolution in order to enable investors, domestic and foreign, to act without concern with respect to rights of ownership of land. Draft legislation on reprivatisation is currently being considered by the Polish Parliament.

The process of 'communalisation' is an important factor in the changes taking place. This involves the transfer of state property to the local self-governing communities (*Gminy*).

## PRIVATISATION

The Privatisation Law came into force in August 1990. It has led to a number of stock exchange flotations, trade sales to domestic and foreign buyers, joint ventures, and 'liquidations' of small and medium-sized enterprises often resulting in the sale or lease of the assets of the enterprise to the employees and/or the management.

An important part of the process of privatisation in Poland is the mass privatisation programme ('MPP') which was finally enacted in May 1993. It involves a scheme for share ownership in which all adults are eligible. A large number of state enterprises will become part of this scheme and will be held by a number of closed-end investment funds (National Investment Funds – NIFs). The key concepts of the scheme are now described.

- ■ Many state-owned enterprises have already been selected and transformed into joint stock companies owned 100 per cent by the state treasury. They are being chosen from among the larger, more economically viable enterprises that have agreed to participate in the programme. A further tranche is awaited at the time of writing.

- Approximately 15 NIFs will be created in the form of joint stock companies. The state treasury will then distribute 60 per cent of its shares in the former state-owned enterprises to the NIFs and another 15 per cent to the employees of those companies. The shareholding in each company participating in the MPP will be as follows:
    - 33 per cent of its stock will be held by a so-called 'leading' or 'dominant' NIF;
    - 27 per cent of the stock will be held by the other NIFs in approximately equal amounts so that each will hold no more than 1–2 per cent of the company's shares;
    - up to 15 per cent will be held by employees of the company (distributed to them free of charge);
    - 25 per cent initially will be retained by the state treasury.

- The NIFs will be administered by management firms which have been selected by way of a competitive tender. Those firms will be charged with the primary task of increasing the long-term value of the funds in which they are dominant shareholders.

- For approximately one year, all shares in the NIFs will be held by the state treasury. After that, share certificates (known as universal share certificates), representing the right to acquire shares in the funds, will be distributed to the Polish public and a fee will be charged. Special share certificates known as compensation share certificates will be issued to certain classes of state employees and pensioners, for which there will be no fee. Eventually, it will be possible to trade shares in individual NIFs on the Warsaw Stock Exchange.

An EBRD draft programme exists for the privatisation of enterprises which have financial difficulties. This programme still requires Polish government and EBRD approval. It will be funded to a large extent by the EBRD.

Privatisation in the more general sense means not just the sale of state assets but also the creation of a private sector. There are many indicators that suggest the private sector in Poland is increasingly active. Official statistics, however, do not tell the whole story and it is difficult to assess the exact strength of the private sector. It is nevertheless instructive to look at some figures; for example, in 1989 the number of private firms was 11,693 and this increased to approximately 41,450 by September 1991; the number of individual establishments increased over the same period from 813,000 to approximately 1.4 million. The overall share of the private sector in GDP is at the time of writing between 45 per cent and 50 per cent; in the retail trade it is 90 per cent; in construction, 77 per cent. As at 1993 the private sector employed 60 per cent of the labour force. These trends can only continue.

## EUROPEAN TRADE

Meanwhile Poland is pursuing its long-term goal of membership of the European Union (EU). As part of this an Association Agreement was signed with the EU in December 1991. The agreement deals with many matters in addition to trade issues and talks of the free movement of workers and capital and rights of establishment. In the short-term the agreement is important for Polish exports for the following reasons:

- some restrictions on Polish exports to the EU were lifted immediately;
- other restrictions will be adjusted over a five-year period; and
- Poland is not required to free up its markets fully until 1999.

Pursuant to this agreement tariffs on 50 per cent of Poland's industrial exports were removed in 1992 and Poland removed tariffs on approximately 27 per cent of EU industrial goods. The remaining tariffs will be removed from both sides over a period of time. There are, however, a number of 'sensitive' products listed in the agreement which are not covered by the short or medium-term liberalisation theme of the document. Such products include iron and steel, coal, textiles and agriculture. Poland is permitted to introduce protective measures in the case of industries undergoing restructuring.

During the Socialist era trade within the Comecon block took place through bilateral agreements and the use of transferable roubles. In 1992 this system had broken down and trading became more commercial. The position with Russia and the members of the former Soviet Union remains confused, as it is not always clear whether and how trade bodies can enter into contracts and whether they are able to obtain foreign currency. Because of the loss of these markets Poland has entered into economic co-operation agreements with some of the new republics, namely Russia, Ukraine, Byelorussia and Latvia.

## CONCLUSION

Another important theme of the Association Agreement with the EU is the requirement of Poland to 'approximate' its laws to those of the EU. The agreement lists a number of areas of law for this purpose including those relating to company law, banking law, company accounts, intellectual property, financial services, competition, consumer protection, indirect taxation and the environment. Legislation can therefore be expected in all these areas. The EU has agreed to provide assistance with respect to seminars, training, provision of experts, translation of EU legislation etc.

Changes have already been made to conform with EU standards: one of the first examples of this was the enactment of the Public Trading in Securities and Trust Funds Act of 22 March 1991. EU directives were used as a basis for this law and for the subsequent amendments made in December 1993. Other examples include the introduction of value added tax legislation, the new copyright law and the law on accounting. Further laws are in the drafting stage, such as a new company law which will create a legal framework for companies based on the European model.

It is clear that there can be no turning back on the path that Poland has embarked on over the last four years. There are many signs that the free market reforms of this period have worked. The private sector continues to grow. There are no longer any shortages; inflation has been brought under control and the convertibility of the zloty has been maintained. Foreign trade is expanding and the integration of Poland into the economy of the wider world is developing. There is an impressive list of foreign companies, including those from the UK who have invested in Poland.

Considering the size of the country compared to its neighbours to the south Poland should attract a continuing larger share of foreign investment. Companies will realize the need to establish and/or protect their market share in a country approaching 40 million people with the potential of accessing the EU market to the West and the emerging economies to the East.

# 5

# Polish Business Culture
## BMF International Ltd

## INTRODUCTION

In order to gain an insight into current Polish business culture, it is essential to understand the historical perspective of carrying out business in Poland, especially in light of the tremendous changes that have occurred in the country over the past four years. Most importantly it is critical to understand the paradigm shift that has transpired in the former Communist region which has resulted in a move away from state controlled command systems towards supply and demand driven free market economies.

For over 40 years after the Second World War Poland was run as a centrally planned system. The most obvious legacy of this time was that enterprises operating in this environment behaved largely as passive production facilities. Other distortions in business created by the Communist regime were: the poor development of infrastructure (telecommunications, roads etc); the establishment of ineffective and inefficient distribution channels; the non-existence of marketing departments; a lack of financial accountability; and inadequate division of management responsibilities. Over the past few years, however, the Polish business culture has changed rapidly, especially with the sudden advent of a burgeoning private sector which now contributes over 60 per cent to GDP. This successful reorientation towards a Western style approach to business in Poland is certainly being helped by the attitude of the Polish people, who have historically always considered themselves part of the West, readily identifying with Western values and regarding Poland as almost the last frontier. It is against this backdrop of recent historical and cultural changes therefore that one needs to interpret current Polish business culture.

### The role of the company in the local community

In the past it was often the case that one company would be the main employer in a town and the prosperity of the area would be closely tied with the fortunes of the company. However, a company's social responsibilities would not end there, but would also often include: the provision and upkeep of a significant proportion of housing in the area; the supply of heat to the town through a hot water ring main from the factory's boiler; upkeep of the local workers' hotel; the provision and maintenance of the local schooling facilities; and building and upkeep of other regional social amenities, such as the local house of culture or swimming pool. Consequently, the managing director of such a company was likely to have authority and responsibilities far wider than would be expected of a director in a similar company in the West. This role of the company in the local community also goes some way to explain the patriarchical attitude a managing director may have to his workforce, as often as not he has been instrumental in employing whole generations of families – and probably still lives among his workforce. Can this be seen as capitalism with a social conscience?

## Character of the Polish workforce

Throughout history Poles have been subjected to decades of repression, and this has been instrumental in helping them strongly unite under a common culture and set of values. This semi-permanent state of oppression has left Poles as romantic idealists with frustrated energy which needs to be channelled and directed carefully as either they can be one's best ally or, if crossed, one's worst enemy.

During these repressive regimes, the Polish people learnt the art of survival by being entrepreneurial and good wheeler-dealers. A good illustration of this dynamism and opportunism is the huge number of traders who made significant profits as the trade barriers were lifted with the West in 1989/90. Accordingly, it is this Polish 'entrepreneurial spirit' that goes a long way to explaining why Poland today has made such huge and rapid strides in reorientating itself towards a free market economy and become the fastest growing economy in Europe.

## Historic work ethic

The centrally planned system did not imbue employees, be they management or staff, with any deep sense of identity with, or responsibility for, their enterprises. In the vast majority of cases work was seen as a means to an end, ie earning money to exist. There was, therefore, no incentive at all to become involved in one's job. This attitude, coupled with the traditional working day being set as 7 am until 3 pm, in most cases resulted in the company being deserted by 3.05 pm. However, as employees realise that the success of their company and their job security lies in their own hands, attitudes are steadily changing and they are becoming more involved in their own work. There is no doubt that this change is also being helped by the steadily increasing number of companies being floated to the public on the Warsaw Stock Exchange. These new, publicly quoted companies are quickly becoming aware of their new accountability, duty and responsibility towards their shareholders.

The question of motivation and instilling a business culture that is geared towards profit maximisation – not, as in the past, fulfilling production quotas – is still the key area which needs to be carefully addressed in any venture in Poland.

## Practicalities in doing business

Poles are a proud nation but quite sensitive to the way they are treated and often a deal can be accepted or rejected at the first meeting. Here are some points which are worth remembering.

- Poles are quite courteous (if you are a woman, do not be surprised to have your hand kissed). Poles are also fairly formal, and usually use titles to show their status and relationship between themselves. Taking an example of an employee called, for instance, Director Jan Nowak, the hierarchy of addressing him would be: Mr Director, Mr Nowak, Mr Jan or Jan, depending on the status and relationship of the other party. There is a large gap in formality between each of these ranks and both parties need to agree mutually to drop to a more informal form of address – otherwise offence can be taken!

- Do not confuse naïvety with stupidity. Much damage has been done by foreigners not remembering Poland's recent history and confusing a lack of modern management expertise with ignorance. One needs to remember however that although nearly half a century of communism has left Polish companies in desperate need of Western know-how and capital, they do have the advantage of having strong business relationships and contacts with the East, and a shrewd and patient understanding of how to operate in what can still be regarded as a somewhat bureaucratic and frustrating business environment. In many cases it is very difficult to do business without a Polish partner who knows how to operate in the current political and economic climate.

- The Communist system did not instill any sense of urgency. Therefore do not be surprised if meetings overrun or appointments run late.

- Patience is key, especially when dealing with any form of local or central government administration. There have been numerous changes in business laws within a small time-frame. These changes happen so quickly that sometimes the new laws leave some ambiguity which local officials find difficulty in interpreting. This problem, combined with a general lack of urgency, often means that working with officialdom can be a lengthy process since no one, it seems, is prepared to take responsibility for decisions.

- In some areas foreigners are still treated with a great deal of suspicion, especially by local authority institutions, who fear that the foreigners will 'grab the best' and Poland's 'crown jewels' will be lost for ever. A partnership approach is highly recommended.

- There is an abundance of statistics and information in Poland, but the poor quality, consistency and interpretation of this data often renders its practical use impossible. Again, having a Polish partner who can navigate through the reams of information and negotiate with ministries and government institutions is almost a necessity.

- The difficulties caused by the disparities between East/West business mentality and the long years of Poles working under a different economic system, should not be underestimated as at times it is difficult to speak the same economic language. There is no doubt that Poles deeply respect Western managers for their financial skills, but these ideas have to be put across carefully, otherwise Poles will feel that they are being patronised.

With Poland's large and indigenous population of 38.6 million and its strategic location as a gateway between East/West trade, there is no doubt that Poland offers tremendous opportunities for investors willing to invest a little patience and flexibility in this most exciting of the new European emerging markets. For investors, a good understanding of the nuances and differences of doing business in Poland is essential. With this knowledge in hand, investors should be able to ensure that any investment made in Poland can be further enhanced by gaining the commitment of a resourceful, well-educated and adaptable workforce – a key asset in creating and sustaining a profitable and successful venture in Poland.

# 6

# Market Intelligence

## BMF International Ltd

### SOURCES OF INFORMATION IN POLAND

In general Poland no longer resembles a blank sheet as far as access to information is concerned. Those sources which existed in the past have been made more customer oriented, and a number of new organisations and companies have been established whose main product is information. Often the problem with information is not its availability but knowing where to find it and persuading the holder to share it.

#### State Agency for Foreign Investment (PAIZ)

The main role of this government body is the promotion of investment in Poland. The agency operates an information centre in the Ministry of Privatisation building in Warsaw. The centre is run by friendly, multilingual staff, and has information on acquisition and joint venture opportunities by industry, region and company size. The centre can also provide information on privatisation laws and procedures.

#### The Main Statistical Office (Główny Urząd Statystyczny – GUS), Warsaw

This is the main national state organisation involved in collecting and processing data. All companies and state enterprises are legally required to submit a standard format balance sheet (F-02) annually, and profit and loss account (F-01) monthly to regional branches of this statistical office. The data are processed and published in various statistical yearbooks which can be bought at reasonable prices. Those which are most attractive to the business community such as the *Industry* or *Foreign Trade Yearbooks* tend to sell out within several months of publishing. The yearbooks contain aggregate data which may be especially useful in market research but do not contain any data on individual companies. Very little of the available information is in English, however, but most of the yearbooks contain contents pages in English and German. The Regional Statistical Offices also publish their own yearbooks.

It is also possible to commission GUS to prepare reports on specific topics. This is now much simpler than previously since there is a customer service desk on the ground floor of the building where written requests for reports can be filed. However, reports on specific companies are not available.

## *Ministries*

Individual ministries no longer have to gather relevant information on their sectors and those that do are usually very unwilling to pass it on. In each ministry there are people who have a very good knowledge of specific industries, but it is not always easy to persuade them to share their knowledge. A good place to start searches are the Foreign Relations Departments which are to be found in most of the ministries.

Some ministries have official publications such as *Privatisation Update* from the Ministry of Privatisation and *Gazeta Przemyslowa* (*Industrial Gazette*) from the Ministry of Industry and Trade which contain information on events relevant to their fields of responsibility.

## *Foreign trade companies*

For information on specific products which were traditionally exported in the past it is worth contacting the foreign trade company which dealt with that item. Since they were responsible for selling and receive feedback from customers, they have a good knowledge of the strengths and weaknesses of specific companies and their products. Most of this information is, however, only available at a price.

## *Specialised companies*

A number of specialist companies, often offering various kinds of market surveys, forecasts and reports, are now in operation. They are usually offshoots of Western companies and offer similar services as would be seen in the West, especially to multinational firms involved in the sales of consumer goods.

## *The press*

Information on the economy, capital markets, specific industries and companies is carried by a number of daily and specialist publications. *Rzeczpospolita* is a daily paper which publishes announcements about tenders organised by ministries and local authorities. It also publishes a monthly called *Businessman* which contains information for the business community. *Nowa Europa* is a 'pink' newspaper which concentrates on economic issues – and even has a back page covering the major stories in

English. The most popular business-related weekly is *Wprost*, whereas publications such as *Życie Gospodarcze* or *Gazeta Bankowa* specialise respectively in the problems of business and finance.

The Polish Press Agency collects press clippings from several daily and weekly publications on a number of current topics. These clippings may be photocopied for a nominal sum. The agency also has its own business news bulletin (*BOSS*) which is published daily and subscriptions are welcome.

## Local authorities

Most provinces (*voivoda*) and even some local authorities (*gmina*) now have Business Development or Economic Activity Departments. Apart from handling privatisations of local companies these departments have extensive information on companies in their region (often in the form of guides and company listings) and are usually more approachable than ministries. They usually have English-speaking staff.

## Libraries

The most interesting sources of information available in libraries are the numerous industry-specific periodicals which are still being published by various institutes. Their quality is mixed with some focusing only on technical issues, whilst others also include market assessments. Although most are available only in Polish the study of several back issues is usually helpful in getting a global idea of a given market.

Recommended libraries include the National Library located a block away from the GUS and the library of the Warsaw School of Economics which is also located nearby. The National Library now operates a computerised catalogue which allows publications to be selected according to specific criteria.

## Institutes

Almost all branches of industry have a corresponding institute, traditionally financed by companies from the sector or the relevant ministry. Currently the role of these institutes has reduced and they are now trying to survive by selling their products. Since they have contacts within the ministries and the business community, they are often able to come up with surprisingly good information in the form of off-the-shelf or specially prepared reports. Such information, however, is rarely available for free.

## Company directories

A number of catalogues listing Polish firms are now in circulation. These range from professional publications such as *Kompass* and *Dun & Bradstreet* guides, and the Business Foundation Books, to small directories published by provincial authorities. They can be bought at good bookstores or directly from the publishers.

## Information about specific companies

This can often be obtained for a fee from Infodata – a department of the National Chamber of Commerce. A standard information package contains information from the court where the company is registered and includes the capital of the company, members of the management and supervisory boards, shareholding structure, assets owned and a credit assessment. The chamber also administers an extensive database which includes offers for co-operation and investment proposals from Polish companies. Also see Appendix 3 for useful addresses.

*Part II*

# The Business Infrastructure

# 7

# Foreign Exchange

## RZB-Austria

### INTRODUCTION

When discussing the transformation of Eastern European economies we often treat Hungary, the Czech Republic, Slovakia and Poland as one bloc. However we should be aware of differences in the pace of reforms in these countries. Poland was the first country in the region to introduce a form of convertibility for its currency, the Polish zloty. This meant a big step forward in facilitating foreign trade and in the development of the banking system.

Before 1989 the zloty was not convertible and importers could buy foreign currencies only through a limited number of state-owned banks. Simultaneously there was a flourishing black exchange market as Poles used to keep their savings in US$ or DM and the only access to Western consumer products they had was through dollar shops (Pewex and Baltona). The 'black' exchange rate was completely different from the official one. In 1989 the authorities decided to legalise the existing situation by permitting the opening of private exchange offices (*kantors*). Simultaneously enterprises effecting their foreign trade transactions through the banks continued to buy foreign exchange at the official (lower) rate.

As a result of the new economic policy of the Polish government the Polish currency became internally convertible in 1990. Its exchange rate was fixed on 1 January 1990 at a level of Zl9500/$US1. This step helped to raise exports and resulted in a considerable surplus in the balance on the current account leading to an accumulation of US$ 5 billion worth of reserves. The Stabilisation Fund organised by the International Monetary Fund remained unutilised. The long-term goal is the full convertibility of the zloty.

Currently the Polish zloty is tied to a basket of five currencies (US dollar, 45 per cent; German mark, 35 per cent; British pound, 10 per cent; French franc and Swiss franc, 5 per cent each). The value of the basket is increased monthly by 1.6 per cent (earlier by 1.8 per cent).

## Exchange controls

The internal convertibility of the Polish zloty means that any private person or legal entity has the right to buy and sell foreign currency.

## External transactions

Although some restrictions remain in force, no limits are currently imposed on the acquisition of hard currency to fund imports of goods and services. The payment has to be done in the currency in which the goods or services had been invoiced and can be effected through any of the licensed foreign exchange banks. The bank, according to Foreign Exchange Control Law, is responsible for checking the documents (commercial invoice) presented by the importer. All hard currency income must be remitted to Poland and exchanged for Polish zloty through one of the licensed banks. Enterprises are not allowed to maintain hard currency accounts abroad or in Poland (although in exceptional cases a special permit can be obtained from the National Bank of Poland). For the time being the European Currency Unit (ECU) is not treated as hard currency, therefore enterprises can maintain ECU accounts in Poland.

Banks in Poland can be divided into three groups:

- banks with a full foreign exchange licence;
- banks with a partial foreign exchange licence;
- banks not authorised to conduct foreign exchange operations.

Currently there are 27 banks with a full foreign exchange licence. Bigger banks authorised for foreign exchange transactions are:

Bank Handlowy, Bank PeKaO SA, Polish Development Bank (PBR), Export Development Bank (BRE), State Savings Bank (PKO BP), Powszechny Bank Kredytowy, Food Economy Bank (BGZ), Bank Slaski, Bank Przemyslowo-Handlowy, Bank Gdanski, Bank Zachodni, Powszechny Bank Gospodarczy, Pomorski Bank Kredytowy, Bank Depozytowo-Kredytowy and a group of banks with foreign capital: Citibank, Societe Generale, ING, Raiffeisen-Centrobank, Creditanstalt, International Bank in Poland (IBP), Amerbank.

## Internal transactions

All business transactions in Poland are denominated in Polish zloty and therefore must be invoiced and settled in local currency. Foreign companies, normally allowed to maintain foreign currency accounts in Polish banks can also have Zl accounts with an appropriate permit.

## Remittance of profits

The state encourages foreign capital investment in Poland as part of an extensive governmental programme of economic reform and development.

The new Foreign Investment Law, effective from 4 July 1991, is applicable to remittances of dividends and capital resulting from investments. The new regulation abolished or eased most of the earlier restrictions on foreign investment in Poland. Capital as well as profits earned in local currency may now be repatriated without special permit.

# 8

# Banking
## RZB-Austria

## THE DEVELOPMENT OF THE BANKING SYSTEM

### The Central Bank

The National Bank of Poland (NBP) is Poland's central bank. It regulates the quantity of money circulating in the economy, sets and controls the level of interest rates, fixes foreign exchange rates based on a basket of major international currencies (US$, DM, £, FFr, SFr) and supervises the whole banking sector. It alone is authorised to issue notes and coins, and acts as the custodian of Poland's foreign exchange reserves.

### The reform of the Polish banking system

The reform of the Polish banking system began in 1989. The former system was structured on a monobank model where the government was responsible for directing refinancing credit to all state-owned enterprises and the role of the central bank was passive (limited to administration of credits etc). In 1987 Poland had only a small number of specialised institutions in addition to the Central Bank. Bank Handlowy specialised in servicing foreign trade transactions, PeKaO SA was conducting retail banking operations in foreign currencies (hard currency accounts of citizens), State Savings Bank (PKO BP) with its extensive network of branches offered retain banking products in domestic currency and Food Economy Bank (BGZ) was the central institution for small co-operative banks serving the agricultural sector.

In 1988 the government decided to reorganise the central bank by forming nine new state-owned commercial banks from NBP's regional branches. The following banks had been created: Powszechny Bank Kredytowy (PBK), Bank Slaski (BSK), Bank Gdanski (BG), Bank Przemyslowo-Handlowy (BPH), Powszechny Bank Gospodarczy (PBG), Bank Zachodni (BZ), Pomorski Bank Kredytowy (PBKS), Bank Depozytowo Kredytowy (BDK) and Wielkopolski Bank Kredytowy (WBK). Those banks took over the assets, liabilities, buildings and the personnel of former NBP branches. Two of them have already been privatised (Wielkopolski Bank Kredytowy and Bank Slaski) and their shares are listed on the Warsaw Stock Exchange. Simultaneously the National Bank of Poland granted a substantial number of banking licences in order to enhance and stimulate competition. Currently there are around 100 licensed banks. There are also over 1500 small local co-operative banks being linked to Food Economy Bank (BGZ). It seems that at present Poland has too many weak, undercapitalised banks which will either have to merge or disappear in the future.

## Banking law

Three Acts are of great importance for the legal environment of banking in Poland:

- the Banking Law of 31 January 1989 and subsequent amendments;
- the Law on the National Bank of Poland of 31 January 1989 and subsequent amendments;
- Foreign Exchange Control Law of 15 February 1989.

## Clearing system

In the previous clearing system the money could be transferred in two ways; either by payment order sent by mail from one bank to another (it even took two weeks to receive funds) or by telegraphic payment order sent by swift, telex or fax. The second solution was quicker (one or two days) but more expensive. However it was preferred by corporate customers due to the high level of interest rates in Poland. Banks prepared a list of postal and telegraphic payment orders sent and received, and delivered them to NBP which effected the clearing. Currently the clearing system is undergoing a process of serious changes.

On 5 April 1993 the National Clearing House (KIR) started its operations. Banks are joining KIR gradually, in groups. By summer 1994 practically all major banks will become KIR members. Although the new system reduced the time factor of money transfers (to a maximum of three days), the clearing is still accompanied by the physical movement of documents. In the second stage a new electronic version of KIR will be implemented, further reducing the time and the quantity of errors. The testing of the electronic system began in the spring of 1994 in a small group of selected banks.

## Interbank market

An active interbank market started in 1992. Now all bigger banks have a dealing room and are connected to the Reuters dealing system. There is only one brokerage company active on the domestic interbank money market: Polish Brokers Company (PBC).

## Money market

Banks are dealing short (overnight, tomnext, spotnext) and longer Zl and hard currency deposits, treasury bills (with maturities of 8, 13, 26, 39 and 52 weeks) and treasury bonds (one and three year). Treasury bills are being sold at primary auctions organised each Monday by NBP. A group of banks which have a status of primary dealers have access to open market operations (repo and reverse repo). Treasury bills are to be dematerialised soon. The level of interest paid on customers' deposits is seriously affected by the high level of obligatory reserves in Poland (23 per cent on demand deposits and 10 per cent on time deposits).

## Foreign exchange market

Banks are permitted to make one deal in one main currency a day with NBP. They deal quite actively among themselves in hard currency against Zl and in hard currency crosses. The market is not very well developed yet and the number of modern products is limited. Only a few banks quote forward contracts (foreign currency against Zl) and options (foreign currency against foreign currency only).

## Deposit insurance

Customers' savings deposits in current and former state-owned banks are guaranteed by the state treasury. However, it is planned to replace the current system with a deposit insurance institution operating on a commercial basis in the form of a joint stock company. The shares will be held by the National Bank, state treasury and banks. The insurance would cover savings and current account deposits.

## Interest rates

Changes in interest rate levels can be illustrated with data concerning National Bank of Poland refinancing credit:

**Table 8.1** *Changing interest rates*

| Period of time | | Refinancing credit |
|---|---|---|
| 1991 | 1 January–31 January | 55 |
| | 1 February–30 April | 72 |
| | 1 May–4 July | 59 |
| | 5 July–1 August | 50 |
| | 2 August–14 September | 44 |
| | 15 September–30 June 92 | 40 |
| 1992 | 1 July–21 February 93 | 38 |
| 1993 | 22 February–12 May 94 | 35 |
| 1994 | 13 May– | 33 |

# 9

# Privatisation

## BMF International Ltd

## INTRODUCTION

One of the fundamental elements of the transformation process of the Polish economy into a free market system has been the privatisation of state-owned enterprises (SOE). At the end of 1990 there were 8453 SOEs (excluding agricultural enterprises). At that time these businesses accounted for 88 per cent of total sales in industry and employed 86 per cent of all employees. By the end of 1993, however, the state-owned enterprises decreased their share in sales and employment to about 60 per cent and 57 per cent respectively.

The legal framework for privatisation is covered by the Privatisation Act and Ministry of Privatisation Act, both passed by Parliament in 1990. Another piece of important legislation is the Act of Foreign Investment in Poland passed in 1989 and amended in 1991.

Privatisation of the SOE is enacted through several basic methods:

### Capital privatisation

At first the SOE is transformed into a state treasury-owned joint stock company (JSC) and then the shares of this newly created company are sold by tender. The decision process is centralised at the level of the Ministry of Privatisation (MoP).

### Winding-up privatisation (privatisation through liquidation)

At first the SOE is struck off the Companies Register. Then, its assets are sold or contributed in kind to a new company. The process is decentralised, decisions are usually taken by founding bodies, such as local government authorities, provincial authorities and ministries other than the MoP.

### Management and/or employee buy-out

At first the employees of a particular SOE set up a limited liability company which subsequently leases the SOE. Lease-to-buy and leveraged-buy-out options (LBO) are used as a way to transfer the ownership from the state treasury to employees. Foreign investors' access to this particular method of privatisation is very limited. The process is decentralised and decisions taken as above.

### Direct foreign investment into SOE or JSC

Sale of assets or joint venture. The process is decentralised. Approval of the MoP and founding bodies is required.

### Mass privatisation programme

About 20 investment capital funds are to be set up to restructure and privatise an initial tranche of around 400 SOEs. The shares of these funds will be available to all Polish citizens over 18 at a very attractive price. The final details of this programme are currently being finalised by the MoP. More information about this programme can be found later in this chapter.

### Liquidation of SOE due to their poor economic and financial condition

These SOEs are liquidated and their assets sold. The process is decentralised. Decisions are taken by the liquidator appointed through the founding bodies (see under 'Winding-up privatisation' above).

In some cases more than one of the procedures mentioned above can be used as the method of privatisation.

## SOME FIGURES ABOUT PRIVATISATION

In the period 1991–3 some 2526 SOEs have undertaken the process of transforming their ownership. This constitutes 30 per cent of the total number of 8453 SOEs operating at the end of 1990 (excluding the agricultural sector)

1. Capital privatisation. In 1992 there was a slowdown in the capital privatisation process. In 1993, despite some improvement in the figures, the total number of transactions completed was far from sufficient to make a substantial impact on the Polish economy.

2. Winding-up and employee buy-outs. Seventy-five per cent of all approved transactions are employee buy-outs (usually a LBO). The majority of SOEs that are leased are small companies with fewer than 200 employees. In general, these types of privatisation have proved to be a tremendous success, with 78 per cent of approved transactions between 1990–3 successfully completed.

**Table 9.1** *Figures about privatisation*

| What has been realised | 1990 | 1991 | 1992 | 1993 | Total |
|---|---|---|---|---|---|
| Capital privatisation | | | | | |
| Transformation of SOEs into JSCs | 38 | 222 | 220 | 47 | 527 |
| Completed privatisations of JSCs | 5 | 22 | 24 | 47 | 98 |
| Winding-up privatisation and employee buy-outs | | | | | |
| Transactions approved | 31 | 418 | 270 | 198 | 917 |
| Transactions completed | 2 | 180 | 293 | 232 | 707 |
| Liquidation of SOE due to poor financial position | | | | | |
| Transactions approved | 18 | 522 | 317 | 225 | 1082 |
| Transactions completed | 0 | 19 | 67 | 86 | 172 |
| Total transactions approved | 87 | 1162 | 807 | 470 | 2526 |
| Total transactions completed | 7 | 221 | 384 | 365 | 977 |

3. The process of liquidating SOEs as a result of their poor financial condition has been a more problematic option for privatisation. Eighty per cent of the transactions approved are for small companies with fewer than 200 employees. Between 1990–3 only 16 per cent of the approved transactions were completed successfully. The main reasons for the low success rate include difficulties in the sale of assets belonging to the liquidated SOEs and the unclear legal status of land and other fixed assets of the SOEs.

In 1991–3 proceeds from privatisation amounted to approximately US$1300 million. The breakdown of the proceeds is as follows.

**Table 9.2** *Breakdown of proceeds*

| Proceeds from | 1991 | 1992 | 1993 | Total | US$ million |
|---|---|---|---|---|---|
| Capital privatisation, privatisation of SOEs, banks and foreign trade companies | 115 | 240 | 240 | 595 | |
| Winding-ups, buy-outs, other | 42 | 130 | 120 | 292 | |
| Total | 157 | 370 | 360 | 887 | |

The above figures do not include the proceeds from the privatisation of Bank Slaski (BSK), which started in 1993 but was completed in 1994. Proceeds from that privatisation amounted to about US$430 million.

## Details of some of the methods of privatisation

*Capital privatisation*

This method of privatisation is mainly used in large JSCs in industry, banking and foreign trade sectors. The shares of JSCs are sold to strategic investors, passive investors (usually foreign institutional investors) or through initial public offerings. In exceptional situations other methods are used, such as MBOs and LBOs.

Capital privatisation is quite sensational since it is widely publicised and attracts small shareholders as well as the attention of the media. For the state treasury it is the most profitable method of privatisation, and as such focuses public attention and evokes many emotions – sometimes including the public perception that Polish assets are being sold off cheaply.

Between 1990–3 the MoP sold 98 JSCs. In addition the shares of three state-owned banks and nine foreign trade companies were also disposed of. According to the law, the employees of privatised companies are entitled to buy up to 20 per cent of shares at a discount of 50 per cent. Just over 50 per cent of JSCs sold were purchased by foreign investors, the remainder by Polish or mixed Polish and foreign consortia. However, the Polish authorities believe that the scope and rate of capital privatisation are insufficient, especially the privatisation of large companies.

Some elements characteristic to transactions involving the sale of JSCs are negotiations on job guarantees, social packages and investment commitments, including environment protection investments. It is, however, difficult to obtain safeguards from the state treasury against possible financial and legal claims from third parties which may only come to light after completion of the transaction. This is mainly because the state treasury does not have contingency funds in the state budget for the compensation of such eventual claims.

The procedure for selling shares of JSCs adopted by the MoP usually follows a similar pattern. The vast majority of M&A services connected with the sale are performed by advisers acting on behalf and under the supervision of the MoP. These advisers, selected on a tender basis, include investment banks, M&A divisions of large consulting companies, law firms and sometimes special plenipotentiaries to the minister. Besides these advisers for individual transactions, some are selected to privatise and/or restructure industrial sectors. Table 9.3 shows these industries and their specific advisers.

In addition some restructuring and privatisation programmes which cover specific industrial sectors are handled by the Ministry of Industry and Trade (MoIT).

### *Mass privatisation programme (MPP)*

Since 1991 work has been carried out on the largest privatisation programme embracing several hundred companies that are to be privatised within one coherent concept. The programme resembles some of the voucher privatisation schemes adopted by other post-communist countries. MPP combines the restructuring and privatisation of companies with the possibility for the mass participation by Polish citizens in the programme through the widespread divestment of ownership in the companies being privatised.

**Table 9.3** *Industries and their advisers*

| Industry | Adviser |
|---|---|
| ■ ball bearings | Kleinwort Benson Ltd |
| ■ breweries | Company Assistance Ltd |
| ■ cables and wires | Bain and Company |
| ■ cement and lime | International Finance Corporation |
| ■ confectionery | Central Europe Trust Co Ltd |
| ■ construction | Company Assistance Ltd |
| ■ electric motors and switch gear | Pro-Invest |
| ■ furniture manufacture | KPMG Peat Marwick |
| ■ glass | Price Waterhouse IPG |
| ■ machine tools | Company Assistance Ltd |
| ■ mechanical and electrical automotive components | Barclays de Zoete Wedd |
| ■ pulp and paper | No adviser at present |
| ■ telecommunications | Bain and Company |
| ■ tyre and rubber manufacture | Societe Generale |

**Table 9.4** *Other industrial sectors*

| Industry | Adviser |
|---|---|
| ■ pharmaceuticals | Boston Consulting Group |
| ■ vehicle manufacturers | Business Management & Finance |
| ■ coal mining | Energy Restructuring Group |
|  | Business Management & Finance |
| ■ iron and steel metallurgy | No adviser at present |

In June 1993 the basic MPP law, ie National Investment Funds (NIF) Law, came into force. It calls for the state treasury to form up to 20 investment funds holding, in total, the shares of several hundred JSCs. Initially the NIFs will themselves be joint stock companies of the state treasury and will be managed by fund managers selected on a tender basis. Next, the shares of NIFs will be distributed among citizens willing to participate in the programme.

In 1993, 367 JSCs were selected for the MPP. Another 100 are expected to be included in the programme this year. The companies themselves decide whether or not to participate in the programme. The preconditions for inclusion, however, are annual sales of at least US$5 million and positive earnings before taxes.

A Selection Committee has been appointed by the MoP to organise an international tender for the fund managers and NIF Supervisory Board members. The invitations to tender were released in September 1993.

In the first quarter of 1994 the Selection Committee selected and recommended to the government 19 fund managers out of 33 candidates. These include foreign and Polish–foreign consortia consisting of investment banks, consulting companies and law firms. At the end of April 1994 the selection of Supervisory Board members for the NIFs was not yet complete.

The timetable for 1994 is to set up the NIFs, appoint the relevant fund managers and Supervisory Boards for the NIFs, and allocate shares of the companies participating in the MPP to the NIFs. Each NIF will be the principal shareholder in some companies, which means having 33 per cent of a company's share capital. Twenty-seven per cent of the remaining share capital of each company will be distributed among all other NIFs. The state treasury shall retain 25 per cent of the shares and the remaining 15 per cent will be distributed free among the employees of a given company.

In 1994 the mass distribution of NIF shares among Polish citizens should begin.

## Programme of privatisation through restructuring

This programme was developed by the MoP in 1993 to utilise the management contract idea in JSCs. The concept is to introduce management groups (MGs) into individual SOEs with the aim of restructuring and later selling the company. MGs are selected through a tender. To win the contract the bidder must submit the best restructuring proposal and offer the highest initial price for the company. The successful bidder pays a financial deposit (4–10 per cent of the initial price) and acquires a call option equal to the deposit. The purpose of the MGs is to restructure and sell the company within a few years to achieve the highest possible capital appreciation. The main component of the MG's fees are: 4–10 per cent of the net annual profit and a commission on the sale of shares in the company to private investors. This commission amounts to 70 per cent of the capital gain in ECU terms. Each MG is free to decide when and to whom to sell the company.

In 1993 invitations for participation in the programme were addressed to state enterprises and to JSCs which met the following criteria:

- not more than 1500 employees;
- clear legal status of the ownership of land and other fixed assets;
- the value of real estate not exceeding US$10 million.

After a selection process 11 companies were chosen. By mid 1994 four management contracts were signed, with several others expected to be completed by the end of the year.

# 10

# Restructuring State Enterprises
## BMF International

### INTRODUCTION

Like most of the countries in Central and Eastern Europe, Poland is also facing restructuring on a macro and micro scale. On the micro scale, company/corporate restructuring in Poland can be broken down into two main areas:

- financial restructuring;
- operational restructuring.

Although the degree to which a company needs to be restructured must be treated on a case-by-case basis, it is useful to explain some of the main historical reasons as to why today so many Polish companies need to be restructured.

### HISTORICAL BACKGROUND

Restructuring in Poland should be taken in context of the dramatic macro-economic changes which the country experienced in early 1990. In January 1990 prices were liberated, virtually all government subsidies on consumer goods were lifted and the money supply was radically reined in. The initial effect was an inflationary shock which only gradually subsided (90 per cent in January, 80 per cent in February etc). The impact of this high inflation was a 30 per cent fall in the standard of living and a dramatic fall in the demand for consumer goods which immediately depressed domestic production. The effect on an average Polish company was devastating.

It must be recognised that prior to 1989/90 most companies in Poland were simply glorified production facilities with their sole concern being to reach centrally dictated production targets. Each company would not worry too much at what cost it achieved these targets (financial control was little more developed than at a book keeping/passive statistical level) and would send its product to specialised trading companies whose responsibility it would be to market and distribute the product to the final client. The impact of the significant macro economic changes at the beginning of 1990 meant the following.

- If a company had a large revolving credit, as many did, then the sudden leap in interest rates would have had a devastating effect on the company's financial position – even though its operations had not changed. (In many instances this was a puzzling situation for the company's management – their financial position had changed and yet their operations were the same!)

- Management were totally unprepared for the fundamental change from a centrally planned economy to a free market system. (The greatest damage caused by the centrally planned system was that it left the majority of Polish companies – especially those in manufacturing – with a false sense of security and naïvety, and with no real concern for competitors nor a sensitivity for their market place.)

- The collapse of the Comecon countries inter-trade gravely affected companies' export markets.

- The downturn in sales was not matched by a downturn in employment as management sought to keep jobs (many Polish towns are based on just one factory).

- The rapid deterioration of sales led to companies becoming cash starved. Initially this was bearable as many companies were overstocked, a legacy of the centrally planned economy during which companies had built up huge stockpiles in fear of running out of materials.

- Companies faced a working capital crunch, therefore they began to strip themselves of working assets and desperately tried to sell or lease surplus social assets in an attempt to pay wages and keep creditors at bay.

- Even worse, companies began to sell below variable costs, simply to generate cash.

- As companies began to face the 'wall' they finally started to make employees redundant, but by this time it was usually too late.

- Even if an upturn in sales came, the company could not respond, as by this time it had chronically weakened its working capital base and had lost any possibility of receiving extended credit from its banks and suppliers because of previous default of payments.

Faced with this catalogue of events, the company would urgently need to be financially restructured, operationally restructured or, commonly, both. In Poland the classic areas to address when faced with restructuring a company are:

- asset reduction, especially non-productive assets such as social clubs, hotels etc;
- improvement in marketing skills;
- cost reduction strategies and cost monitoring systems;
- changes in top management;
- introducing strong cash flow control.

## FINANCIAL RESTRUCTURING

It does not necessarily follow that a company that needs to be restructured is poorly run on a day-to-day basis. Quite often the company may only need to be financially restructured as a consequence of previous poor financial management rather than poor operational management.

The typical approach is to investigate if the company is generating an operating profit. If this is the case, then the financial operations should be examined and, where appropriate, companies can make use of the legal framework set up to aid Polish companies in reducing their debt burdens. Specifically these are as follows.

- The Arrangement Proceedings Act, dated 24 October 1934. If a company is in a position where it is unable to settle its debt repayments to its creditors, then it can apply to the local district court to arrange a rescheduling of its debt. This involves the company in 'opening its books' and putting forward proposals detailing a comprehensive debt rescheduling package. Unfortunately, however, this process can be somewhat complicated since it requires the agreement of at least two-thirds (sometimes more, depending on the reduction conditions) of all the creditors (by debt value) and at least 50 per cent of all creditors (by number, which includes the many, very small suppliers to the company) for the proposal to be implemented. This means, therefore, that in practice it is often extremely difficult to implement the debt rescheduling package using these financial proceedings.

- The Act on the Financial Restructuring of State Enterprises and Banks and Amendments to other legislation, dated 3 February 1993 (Bank Conciliatory Agreement – BCA). Unlike the Arrangement Proceedings Act, the BCA only applies to a company/enterprise in which more than 50 per cent of the shares are directly or indirectly state owned. In general the BCA has so far been the most effective instrument in restructuring companies in Poland, which is surprising since it was supposed to assist more in the restructuring of banks, not companies. However, it has resulted in several hundred companies having to review their strategies, current situations etc, and devising appropriate restructuring programmes. It is still, however, to be seen whether these companies will be able to build on this forced first step and look to a more detailed/deeper restructuring in the future.

The most common financial problems that Polish companies face and need to address are as follows.

## *Asset and liability management*

Polish companies often fall into a debt trap and cannot find a solution alone. This results in companies continuously operating in crisis management, fighting for survival rather developing a future strategy. This also means that the company is operating with the continual threat of bankruptcy. Management find it difficult to separate out core businesses and divest redundant assets, including social amenities.

## *Control over working capital*

In many instances stock control is very poor and there is a lack of appreciation of the cost of money locked up in raw materials. Similarly the management of receivables is often too relaxed, allowing for the accumulation of significant overdue sums, while at the same time continuing to trade with the delinquent clients.

## *Poor capital management*

Management is often not familiar with using different financial instruments which may be available for financing the company. Typically, the only financing available is a zloty-denominated credit carrying a high rate of interest (+35 per cent July 1994). This is partly caused by a shortage of more innovative financial products provided by Polish commercial banks. Little use is made of the opportunity to refinance existing debt, for instance having it denominated in US dollars or Deutschmarks, or changing it from a fixed rate to a floating rate.

## *Lack of information on specific product or department profitability*

The accounting systems in the companies are not designed to give essential information to management. As a result, management cannot identify the variable costs of any particular product, so pricing decisions are based on intuition and on the current full cost system.

## OPERATIONAL RESTRUCTURING

This process should start with an in-depth analysis (current position review) of the company to obtain a precise picture of its current state. This study addresses all the major areas of the company's operations and allows the identification of the most significant problems. In addition, it provides a good understanding of the market position, product quality, production facilities, financial position, management quality, possibilities for debt restructuring, as well as current product profitability.

Some of the typical problem areas, in addition to those mentioned above, are as follows.

### *Lack of marketing skills*

Until recently most international marketing for any company was handled by an independent foreign trade organisation. This has resulted in most managements today lacking the experience and skills required to market their own products. There is often a lack of understanding of the customer needs, market segmentation, competitive positioning etc. Pricing, therefore, is not optimised, products are over or under-designed, packaging is ill-conceived and distribution channels are not optimised. In addition marketing departments are still very under-developed in most organisations, often comprising of only one or two dedicated people. Foreign travel is often still considered a perk and, as such, reserved for the top directors who do not want more junior members of marketing departments to travel.

### *Poor information flow within the company*

Most activities are not computerised within a company, therefore management receives crucial information late or not at all.

### *Lack of correlation between the effects of work and pay*

The typical wage structure in a state-owned company is very flat and so does not motivate employees (and management) to increase productivity or profitability.

## RESTRUCTURING PROGRAMME

In many instances quite radical changes in profitability can be achieved simply through the implementation of basic, sound general management techniques, to ameliorate the problems described above.

Once the problem areas within the company have been identified, a restructuring programme to tackle them is devised and implemented. This is usually done in conjunction with independent consultants and would embrace such elements as:

- introducing tight cash flow controls;
- negotiating better terms with creditors;
- finding strategic partners and trade partners;
- bolstering the marketing department, training where necessary;
- running customer/product/market surveys;
- appraising the activities of competitors;
- defining a new internal organisational structure and information flows;
- assisting in recruiting an appropriate management team;
- examining current technology – does it need updating and how much will it cost;
- introducing cost cutting solutions;
- introducing stock and trade debtor controls;
- introducing computerisation and MIS;
- training management in modern management techniques;
- reappraising the asset portfolio and selling non-productive parts;
- introducing a new pay and promotion system;
- starting a quality control programme etc.

In order to achieve the successful implementation of such a programme Task Force groups are usually formed out of management and employees of the company. These groups work with the consultants on problem identification, joint development of new solutions and their implementation. Frequently it is essential that during the first year an active supervisory role is taken by the consultant to ensure that the implementation process does not falter. Over time, however, leadership of such groups is handed over to the management itself. It is crucial for management to be deeply involved throughout the restructuring process – they need to have not only ownership of the problem, but also the solution. In addition, the Supervisory Board/Workers Council (depending on whether it is a state enterprise or a state-owned joint stock company), as well as employee representatives, would be kept informed on a regular basis.

Typically, the restructuring programme would take into account that the traditional objectives of the company's management were, for instance, to retain employment or maximise production. It is very rare to find companies which are focused on long-term profitability – at least not in state-owned companies. Therefore effective restructuring needs to be connected with ensuring that management selects a suitable set of realistic objectives. In addition, it is strongly recommended that restructuring should be connected with the company's privatisation, otherwise the results can be ineffective as there is no owner to whom to be accountable and no sense of responsibility from the management.

In the near future, the implementation of the mass privatisation programme will result in the effective restructuring of many profitable Polish companies. It is expected that up to 900 companies will enter this programme and will be subject to restructuring by the National Investment Funds.

# 11

# Foreign Investment
## Nabarro Nathanson

## INTRODUCTION

The law regulating foreign investment in Poland is the Law of 14 June 1991 on Companies with Foreign Participation ('the Foreign Investment Law'). Specific laws such as the banking, insurance or telecommunication laws will apply to investments in this area.

The Foreign Investment Law is applicable to non-resident natural or legal persons. Such foreign persons may create and operate enterprises in Poland only in the form of limited liability companies or joint stock companies. They may also purchase and hold shares of such companies already in existence.

## APPROVALS

With the exception of a few strategic areas in the Polish economy, an investment by a foreign person under the Foreign Investment Law does not require any governmental approval; it simply requires registration of the Polish company which is routine for all limited liability or joint stock companies – for the procedure of incorporation see Chapter 28.

### Strategic areas permits

A permit is required when the company intends to engage in one of the following activities:

- management of seaports and airports;
- real estate brokerage and sales;
- any defence industry activities, not covered by separate concessions;
- wholesale trading in imported consumer goods; or
- provision of legal services.

A permit is also required if the other partner is a 'state legal person' (companies wholly-owned by the treasury are excluded), which invests in the initial capital of a company formed under the Foreign Investment Law in the form of a non-monetary contribution such as its own enterprise, a branch or department capable of serving a specific business purpose, or its real estate.

The Ministry of Privatisation issues the permits. The permit issued may contain conditions such as the ratio of Polish to foreign ownership or voting rights in the initial capital.

As mentioned a real estate contribution by a state legal person to a company with foreign participation also necessitates government approval. It is generally accepted that not only a contribution of full ownership of land falls under this provision, but also a transfer of any interest in real estate. This would include the right to a 'perpetual usufruct' (broadly equivalent to a long lease) on land owned by the state treasury or a local self-governing community (*Gmina*).

## Permits related to a foreign interest in an existing company

The approval requirement for foreign participation in companies doing business in areas governed by the Foreign Investment Law could be easily circumvented by subsequent acquisition of the shares in an already established entity. Therefore, the law imposes a permit requirement on certain activities connected to companies that are within the scope of the restricted areas of the economy. A permit is required for any of the following:

- the acquisition of shares or any interest in shares of a company carrying out any restricted activity;
- the expansion of a company's scope of activities into restricted areas; and
- the conclusion of a contract for the use of, for more than six months, real estate, an enterprise or a branch of an enterprise, belonging to a 'state legal entity'.

There is no statutory definition of 'state legal entity'. It is obvious, however, that the term refers to the state treasury, state enterprises and other entities having their 'legal personality' accorded by statute. All companies with private ownership are outside the scope of this definition. The Foreign Investment Law excludes from this concept companies wholly owned by the state treasury.

## Other permits required by specific statutes

A company established under the Foreign Investment Law may be required to obtain concessions, licences or permits under statutes or regulations other than the Foreign Investment Law. Although such concessions are not a prerequisite to the establishment of a company, if a permit is required, the company may not commence the activity in question before it is obtained.

Business activities subject to concessions include, for example, the exploration and exploitation of minerals, the production and sale of explosives, the manufacture of pharmaceuticals and the manufacture of tobacco products.

### *Acquisition of land*

Permission is required from the Ministry of Interior for the acquisition by a foreign person of either a freehold interest or a perpetual usufruct. The requirement stems from the Law of 24 March 1920, which was amended in 1933, 1988 and 1990. The occupational forms of lease, notably *Dzierżawa* and *Najem*, do not generally require such consent. However, as stated above a *Dzierżawa* concluded for more than six months, with respect to the property of a state enterprise, requires a permit from the Ministry of Privatisation under the Foreign Investment Law.

The definition of 'foreign persons' includes individuals who are not Polish citizens, legal entities based abroad and Polish legal entities controlled directly by parties within the previous definitions; in the case of a company, one in which not less than 50 per cent of the capital is controlled by such persons or entities is a foreign person.

The application must specify the name and address of the applicant, full description of the land including its registered details, the purchase price and the status of the land as specified in the economic planning document for the area, as well as a formal valuation. If the acquisition is from a party in respect of which there is a special procedure to determine value, for example where acquisition is from a local authority, the application must demonstrate that the procedure has been correctly followed.

A 'foreign person', having acquired land, is in the same legal position with regard to both rights and obligations, as a Polish citizen or company.

## PROTECTION OF FOREIGN INVESTORS

A company formed under the Foreign Investment Law is a Polish legal entity, established under Polish law. Therefore, the foreign investor in such an entity is protected against expropriation of private property by the Polish Constitution. One of the post-Communist amendments to the Constitution, passed on 29 December 1989, established the principle of state protection and guarantees for private property.

Expropriation can still, of course, occur for a public purpose and for just compensation. Otherwise private property is fully protected.

The Foreign Investment Law contains specific protection against expropriation of foreign investment, in addition to the constitutional one.

The law provides that the foreign investor has a right to compensation for its share of the company's assets and for damages sustained as a result of direct or indirect expropriation. Further forms of protection for foreign investors are to be found in bilateral investment protection treaties entered into by Poland with a number of countries including most Western European countries and the USA.

## SOURCE OF CAPITAL INVESTED IN A COMPANY FORMED UNDER THE FOREIGN INVESTMENT LAW

The Polish currency is not fully convertible. The internal convertibility of the zloty is protected by a number of exchange control restrictions contained primarily in the Foreign Exchange Law of 15 February 1989 and the various regulations issued under it.

The Foreign Investment Law also contains certain provisions dealing with foreign currency. The foreign investor will pay in zloty for its shares in a Polish company; share capital cannot be expressed in a foreign currency. Such currency, however, must originate from the sale of foreign currency at a Polish bank authorised to deal in hard currency transactions.

A foreign investor may purchase its share in the company with money not originating from the exchange of hard currency. For example, the money may come from income earned in Poland by another company formed under the Foreign Investment Law or in another form approved by the Ministry of Finance.

Foreign currency loans to a Polish company require a permit from the National Bank of Poland.

## REPATRIATION OF PROFITS

The Foreign Investment Law permits full transfer of profits abroad. Before profits may be remitted corporate income tax must be paid. The profit is paid in Polish currency but the law provides the foreign investor the right to purchase foreign currency in a foreign exchange bank for the amount paid to it by the company on account of its share of profits. In order to obtain the foreign currency, a certificate on the annual accounts must be produced from the auditors of the company. The foreign party can then transfer abroad without a separate foreign exchange permit the foreign currency purchased in the foreign exchange bank.

The ability to repatriate proceeds from Poland in hard currency applies also to the following:

- amounts received from the sale or redemption of company shares;
- amounts due in case of liquidation of the company; and

- amounts obtained as compensation on account of expropriation, direct or indirect.

The employees of a company formed under the Foreign Investment Law who are foreign persons have the right, after the payment of any taxes due, to purchase foreign currency in a foreign exchange bank with the Polish currency earned from employment. A certificate issued by the company is sufficient to authorise the employee to conduct the exchange transaction. Repatriation of such earnings does not require any separate foreign exchange permit.

## REPRESENTATIVE OFFICES

Branches of foreign companies are regulated by the 1976 Council of Ministers regulation on 'representative offices'. This regulation is expected to be replaced.

A representative office does not have a separate legal personality. The scope of activity of a company conducting business through a representative office is limited to foreign trade, transportation, tourism and entertainment services. A representative office may take one of three statutory forms:

- a branch or an agency;
- a technical information office;
- a contract supervision office.

A branch may only carry on such business that is within the objects of the parent company. Conduct of certain business activities by a branch may be limited either by the permit issued, or by Polish commercial, tax or foreign exchange laws. A technical information office may be established for the purpose of providing information. A contract supervision office may be set up to supervise the performance of particular contracts.

In order to establish a representative office a foreign company must obtain a permit from the minister of foreign economic co-operation. This permit is issued for a limited period (currently two years) and must be renewed prior to expiration. An application for the permit must include the company's memorandum and articles of incorporation (or other constitutive document), a statement of its intent to establish a representative office and an undertaking to observe Polish laws, all of which must be certified by an appropriate consular office and filed together with a Polish translation.

## 12

# Capital Markets

## BMF International Ltd

There was no capital market in post-war Poland prior to the economic reforms undertaken by the first non-Communist government which came to power in 1989. Personal wealth was held mainly in bank deposits (denominated in both zloties and foreign currencies) and in cash. Finance for industry was provided through short-term credits or medium-term loans by the National Bank of Poland, which, until its restructuring in 1989, combined the functions of a central bank and a commercial bank. Finance for the agricultural sector was provided through a network of over 1200 small co-operative banks.

Having set itself the objective of transforming the socialist economy to a free market one, the new government was faced with the task of creating the institutions and instruments to facilitate the development of a capitalist system. The development of the equity, bond and money markets is discussed below.

## EQUITIES

### The regulatory framework

The Act on Public Trading and Trust Funds of 22 March 1991 sets the legal framework for securities trading and the activities of trust funds in Poland. The Act also established the Securities Commission, endowing it with overall responsibility for security trading. Public trading in any security requires the approval of the Securities Commission. An amendment to the Act, which was passed in 1993, aims to strengthen the integrity of the market, and established fines for insider trading and attempts to manipulate share prices. It also imposes reporting requirements when share ownership reached 5 per cent and other higher trigger points.

### The Warsaw Stock Exchange

After its closure in 1939, the Warsaw Stock Exchange (WSE) was formally reopened on 16 April 1991. Owned jointly by its 23 members, comprised of banks, brokerage houses and the state treasury, the exchange is located at the Warsaw Banking Centre in what used to be the Communist party headquarters.

The new stock exchange had a slow start. By December 1991, five stocks had been listed, all of which were issued through a public flotation under the government's privatisation programme. Activity did not pick up until the end of 1992, but 1993 saw a very rapid expansion of companies seeking a listing and of investor interest. Twenty-four companies (including one on the so-called 'parallel' market) were listed by the end of June 1994.

Investor interest grew rapidly in 1993. The change of sentiment was created partly by a reduction in interest rates available on bank deposits and partly by the growing recognition of the stock market's potential. The latter feeling was reinforced by the sharp increases in the stock market index ('WIG') in the early part of 1993, at which time the WSE attracted also the interest of foreign investors.

The boom continued throughout 1993 and into the first quarter of 1994. The WIG index rose from 1037 at the start of 1993 to a peak of 20,760 in March 1994. The rapid price increases pushed p/e ratios of many companies beyond 50. Inevitably, the bubble burst and the second quarter of 1994 saw a dramatic drop, with the WIG index reaching a low point of 7215 in June 1994.

By the end of June 1994 the WIG index had recovered slightly to 7922. At that point, total market capitalisation of the listed companies was Zl59.5 trillion, equivalent to £1.7 billion.

## *Listing requirements*

Admission of new securities to the WSE requires approval from the Securities Commission. This requires the preparation of a prospectus, containing at least three years' financial information. Other requirements include:

- value of issuers shares to be not less than Zl20 billion;
- at least 20 per cent of the shares to be made available for public offering;
- unlimited transferability of the shares.

The WSE provides also for a parallel market with less rigorous listing requirements, though only one company has taken advantage of this to date.

Once admitted, issuers must provide audited annual statements, semi-annual reviews and quarterly unaudited reports.

## *Broking companies*

Transactions on the WSE are carried out through broking companies, of which 35 had been licensed by the end of 1993. Most of these companies are subsidiaries of the major banks, whose branches serve as distribution points to the investing public. Trading is conducted three times a week, on Mondays, Tuesdays and Thursdays; there are plans to introduce daily trading by the end of 1994.

Shares listed on the WSE are all in bearer form and dematerialised, being held at the National Deposit for Securities, an electronic central share register. Persons wishing to trade on the WSE must have an 'investment account' with a licensed bank or broking company. The trading system is based on computerised orders from the broking firms, that determine the price at which supply and demand for any security are balanced. However, the price may not move by a margin of more than 10 per cent in either direction in any one session and trading in a security is suspended if this margin were to be breached.

It is estimated that there are currently over 800,000 investment accounts in operation. Over 400,000 were created for the purposes of the much publicised privatisation of Bank Slaşki in February 1994. Daily turnover has been rising rapidly, and by December 1993 averaged 56,000 trades. Eighty-six thousand trades were recorded in one session in January 1994, approaching the levels of the New York Stock Exchange.

## *Capital raising*

The WSE was utilised initially as a vehicle for the government's privatisation programme, proceeds of the flotations flowing mainly to the state treasury. However, the growth of the market in 1993 prompted several companies to raise capital through the WSE. These included new issues from companies such as Elektrim SA, Exbud SA and Swarzędź SA, which had been earlier privatised by flotation, as well as by private companies, such as the Bank Inicjatyw Gospodarczych SA, which was established as a private sector bank in 1989.

## *Investment funds*

Pioneer is the first and, to date, the only mutual fund (unit trust), operating in Poland. Its portfolio is split between WSE-listed shares and government bonds, with up to 10 per cent invested overseas. By June 1994, Pioneer had registered over 500,000 investors and managed on their behalf a portfolio worth over Zl21 trillion.

A number of offshore 'emerging market' funds have also been active on the WSE. Several specialist investment funds, both offshore and Polish, are expected to be launched during 1994 targeting listed and unlisted companies in selected industrial sectors.

# BONDS

## *Government bonds*

Until 1992, the budget deficits were financed through the banking system, mainly through the issue of treasury bills. The first public issue of government bonds took place in June 1989, when a total of Zl600 million was offered to the public. This was followed by a planned issue of Zl5 billion, repayable on 31 December 2000. Offering interest equal to the rate of inflation during the first five years, and 3 per cent pa fixed thereafter, it was aimed mainly at investors planning to participate in the privatisation programme by allowing them to use the bonds in payment for the shares, while obtaining a 20 per cent price discount. The bonds were available to investors until April 1991, but the take-up proved very low.

In 1991 the government issued US dollar denominated debt and offered it to the major banks in settlement of outstanding government liabilities. This assisted the banks in balancing their currency exposures created by the substantial foreign currency deposits, which still remains a popular form of savings in the personal sector. The bonds were issued in 25 series, totalling US$5453 million, with repayment between 1 April 1992 and 1 April 2004.

In June 1992 the government launched the first offering of one-year treasury bonds. This totalled Zl8 trillion, and was issued in 4 series over a 12-month period. In June 1993, an issue of four further series, totalling Zl14 trillion was announced. Interest is paid on maturity and is calculated at 5 per cent per annum over the actual rate of inflation, as measured by the movement in the official inflation index during the 12-month period commencing in the second month prior to the date of issue.

In August 1992 the government commenced issuing three-year bonds. Although a total of Zl7 trillion and Zl8 trillion were planned for 1992/3 and 1993/4 respectively, actual sales up to December 1993 totalled under Zl2.5 trillion. Interest is payable quarterly and is calculated by applying a fixed coefficient (110 per cent on current bonds) to a base rate. The base rate for each quarterly period is the average yield on 13-week treasury bills obtained at the last 4 treasury bill auctions preceding the start of the relevant interest period.

In May 1994 the government issued the first fixed interest bonds, for two and five years, maturing on 12 June 1996 and 12 June 1999 respectively. Interest on the bonds is payable annually, and accrues at the rate of 18 per cent pa on the one-year bonds and 15 per cent pa on the three-year bonds.

Government bonds are traded on the WSE, though brokerage houses may also trade them outside the exchange, subject to permission from the Securities Exchange. Transactions over Zl10 billion may be conducted also on the inter-bank market.

## Municipal bonds

Several local authorities started issuing bonds in 1993, including the Warsaw district of Mokotów and the municipality of Plock. Despite inducements, such as discounts on assets purchased from the local authorities under privatisation programmes, these bonds have not proved popular and issues were not fully placed. Although such bonds can be traded through local brokers, in practice they are very illiquid.

## Corporate bonds

On account of the prevailing high interest rates, no medium-term bonds have yet been issued, although several listed companies have considered the possibility of issuing convertible bonds. Some of the listed companies, such as Elektrim, Mostostal Warszawa, Tonsil and Swarzędź have issued Commercial Paper. These are negotiable instruments with a maturity not exceeding one year and are issued at a discount to nominal value. In the absence to date of investors in this market, the Commercial Paper issues have been taken up by the sponsoring banks. The Polish Development Bank, which quotes buying and selling prices on a daily basis for the issues it has sponsored, and Bank Przemyslowo-Handlowy in Kraków are the most active institutions in this field.

# MONEY MARKETS

## Treasury bills

Treasury bills have been used traditionally to finance the budget deficits. Since May 1991 the National Bank of Poland has organised weekly auctions in the money market. Treasury bills are currently issued in denominations of Zl100 million, 1 billion and 10 billion, and for maturities of 8, 13, 26, 39 and 52 weeks.

## Certificates of deposit

The Polish Development Bank (PDB) was the first and is still the only significant issuer of certificates of deposit (CD). It operates programmes covering one-month zloty-denominated CDs, and three-month currency and currency-indexed CDs. Zloty-denominated CDs are issued with a nominal value of Zl1 billion, while currency CDs are issued with nominal values of $50,000 or 100,000 currency units in any other major currency. PDB CDs are quoted daily, and the PDB organises a secondary market in these securities. Bank Śląski was the first commercial bank to issue its own CDs.

## The inter-bank market

Tradition and inadequate fund transfer mechanisms retarded the development of an inter-bank market until 1992. Over the past two years, however, the market has grown significantly, with the level of inter-bank deposits exceeding Zl20 trillion by the end of 1993, more than double the level of 18 months previously. The Warsaw Interbank Offer and Bid Rates (WIBOR and WIBID) are quoted daily for maturities of overnight, 'tomorrow night', 'spot-night', one week, two weeks, one month, two months and three months. The foreign-owned banks play a particularly significant role in this market. Most transactions are carried out directly between the banks' treasury departments, though broking services are provided by the Polish Development Bank and by a specialist broking company, Polish Brokers Limited.

The National Bank of Poland plays an increasingly important role in controlling the liquidity in the market through open-market operations. It purchases and sells qualifying securities from and to the market by offering repo and reverse-repo programmes.

# 13

# Valuation and Accounting

## *Deloitte & Touche, Warsaw*

The accounting regulations which apply to entities operating in Poland were set out by a decree issued by the Minister of Finance of 15 January 1991, and took effect for accounting periods starting from 1 January of that year. They are universal in application and apply equally to state owned as well as privately owned enterprises, and to companies with foreign participation set up under the joint venture law.

The accounting rules are closely linked to Poland's tax law, and entities' statutory accounts are generally the same as those used for tax purposes. While most of the accounting principles are laid down in the accounting regulations, one exception is the definition of fixed assets and the setting of depreciation rates which is the responsibility of the Council of Ministers.

After introductory sections on reporting requirements and accounting practices, this chapter explains the main accounting and valuation policies used in Poland, together with audit requirements for Polish companies.

## REPORTING REQUIREMENTS

All limited liability companies and joint stock companies must file their financial statements at the Commercial Register and Tax Office. The accounting year, as well as the tax year, for Polish companies is generally the calendar year to 31 December, however this may be changed on application to the authorities. A company's financial statements must be approved by a meeting of the shareholders; within six months of the accounting year end for a limited liability company, and four months for a joint stock company, and filed at the Registration Court and Tax Office within two weeks of the date of approval. Companies which are required to have an audit must also file a copy of their audit report.

The financial statements comprise a balance sheet and profit and loss account. In addition, a statement setting out the following details must be produced by large companies:

- the company's financial standing;
- anticipated future developments including details of research and development projects and investment programmes;
- details of fixed asset movements;
- the amount and type of the company's share capital;
- the nominal value of any own shares purchased during the year;
- the liquidity of the company;
- details of the company's personnel.

These details are not required for small businesses which need only prepare a simplified balance sheet and profit and loss account. A business is defined as small if two out of the following requirements are met:

- there are no more than 50 employees; *and*
- the balance sheet total in the previous accounting period was less than Zl 30,000,000,000; *and*
- turnover in the previous accounting period was less than Zl 120,000,000,000.

## ACCOUNTING PRACTICES

The accounting regulations require that entities keep current and accurate records, and they describe in detail the bookkeeping to be carried out by companies and the documents which may form a basis of the accounting entities. Records must be kept in the Polish language and in Polish currency, and they must be based on a chart of accounts established by the management of the enterprise.

## ACCOUNTING POLICIES

The accounting policies set out under Poland's accounting regulations generally comply with the concepts established in the EEC's fourth directive on company law, although there are certain marked exceptions, such as the absence of any requirement for holding companies to produce consolidated accounts or to disclose the existence of their subsidiaries, and the absence of any disclosure of transactions with related parties. Where entities operate as a number of divisions they are required to produce consolidated accounts, ie one return for the whole legal entity.

### *Depreciation*

Fixed depreciation rates which apply to all taxpayers are established by the

Council of Ministers. There are a number of rates in the range 1.5 per cent to 50 per cent, which are generally applied on a straight line basis. Sample rates are 2.5 per cent to 4 per cent for buildings, 8.5 per cent to 20 per cent for plant and machinery and 10 per cent to 20 per cent for intangible assets.

The rates given may be doubled for assets in certain groups, mainly plant and machinery and means of transportation with the exception of passenger cars, which were taken into an entity's books after 1 January 1991. A threefold increase is possible if the assets concerned are used in an area of structural unemployment. This accelerated depreciation is calculated on a reducing balance basis.

## Revaluation of assets

Most fixed assets are subject to compulsory revaluations which are decreed from time to time by the Minister of Finance. Depreciation, using the rates set out above, is then based on the revalued amount.

## Intangibles

Intangible assets, including goodwill, may generally be capitalised if they are acquired as a direct purchase. Goodwill is calculated as the excess of the purchase price of an enterprise over its net book value, and is written off over a period up to five years. Other intangibles are recorded separately at cost and are amortised at variable rates. The costs of raising share capital are included in intangible assets in a joint stock company, but not in a limited liability company.

## Leased assets

The accounting regulations distinguish between operating leases and finance leases. The former are effectively treated as rental agreements, and the latter as purchase agreements. Payments made under the former are treated as revenue earning costs at the time that they are made, while assets held under finance leases are capitalised in the lessee's books and depreciated over the period of the lease term. Classification of leases is made on the basis of specific rules issued by the Ministry of Finance on 6 April 1993. In general a lease will be regarded as a finance lease if it includes an option to buy for the lessee.

## Research and development costs

Research and development costs are generally capitalised, and depreciated over the life of the product to which they relate.

## Capitalised interest

Interest payments related to the construction of own assets may be capitalised, together with any other ancillary costs related to construction.

These are then written off once the asset concerned is bought into use, using the depreciation rate which applies to it.

### *Inventory valuation*

Inventories are valued at the lower of cost and net realisable value. Costs may be established using LIFO, FIFO, or a standard cost or weighted average basis. Long term work in progress is valued either at cost or at an appropriate percentage of final sales value, which may include an element of unrealised profits. There is no requirement for immediate recognition of anticipated losses on long term contracts.

### *Deferred taxation*

There are no provisions in the accounting regulations concerning deferred tax accounting. This would generally not be required as most differences between income for accounting and income for tax purposes are of a permanent nature.

### *Foreign exchange*

All transactions effected in foreign currency are recorded in zloty using the exchange rate established by the National Bank of Poland for the date of the transaction. Exchange differences are disclosed as income or costs related to financial transactions. Any items outstanding at the year end are translated at the year end rate. Unrealised exchange losses are written off directly to the profit and loss account, while unrealised gains are taken to deferred income.

### *Investments*

All investments, both long term and short term, are stated at the lower of cost or market value. There is no requirement to provide details of investments held, or to disclose the existence of subsidiaries.

## AUDIT REQUIREMENTS

Auditing in Poland is governed by the law of October 1991 on Auditing and Publications of Financial Statements and Certified Accountants, which came into force on 1 January 1992.

An audit is obligatory in Poland for all joint stock companies, state owned enterprises, limited liability companies which are more than 50 per cent state owned and banks and insurance companies. Other companies must be audited if two out of the following three criteria were met in the preceding year:

- ■ average employment over the year exceeded 50 people; *or*

- total assets or total liabilities exceeded 1,000,000 ECU; *or*
- turnover during the year exceeded 2,000,000 ECU.

In addition, companies with foreign participation are required to have their financial statements audited if they wish to transfer their profits for the year abroad as a dividend. Most companies with foreign participation require audited financial statements which comply with international standards for their shareholders, in addition to the audited accounts produced for the Polish authorities.

Auditing firms are licensed by the National Auditing Board. There is no maximum period of appointment for them.

## *Note*

At the time of going to press new laws on Accounting and Auditing were passed by the lower chamber of parliament (Sejm) but had yet to be passed by the upper chamber of parliament (Senate) and accepted by the President. The changes announced are not reflected in this chapter.

The law on accounting which will come into effect on 1 January 1995 will bring sweeping changes to the Polish accounting standards as it will bring them into line with international standards. In particular it will introduce the consolidation of accounts for groups of companies and it will enable entities to establish their own depreciation and amortisation policies. It will also result in the introduction of accounting for deferred taxation.

# 14

# The Fiscal Regime

*Deloitte & Touche, Warsaw*

The system operating in Poland is no longer based on the separate taxation of public and private sectors. State entities no longer have advantages over other entities. The principal Act regulating the carrying out of business in Poland is the Act of 1988 on Economic Activities. The Act provides that economic activity may be carried on by any person, on equal terms, subject to the conditions specified under provisions of the Polish Law. A subject carrying on economic activity may be a natural person, a legal person or an organisational unit having no legal personality.

In general, any individual or entity earning an income is subject to tax. Legal entities including limited liability companies and joint stock companies are subject to corporate income tax on their profits. Entities such as civil partnerships, registered partnerships and limited partnerships do not have legal personality, and their participants are subject to personal income tax on their individual shares in the profits of the entity.

After an introductory section on the Polish tax authorities this chapter explains the main taxes applicable to individuals and companies.

The principal taxes are:

- corporate income tax;
- individual income tax;
- value added tax;
- social insurance obligations;
- real property tax;
- agricultural tax;
- stamp duty.

## THE TAX AUTHORITIES

The tax authorities operate on three levels. The highest is the Ministry of

Finance, below which are the Fiscal Chambers, and then the Tax Offices. Taxpayers deal in the first instance with the Tax Offices which:

- calculate and collect taxes;
- act as a court of first instance in tax cases;
- enforce administrative decisions regarding financial liabilities;
- exercise fiscal control.

Administrative cases are generally heard in two stages. Appeals against decisions made by the Tax Offices may be made to the relevant Fiscal Chamber. In exceptional cases however, further appeals are possible, to the High Administrative Court on points of law, or to the Ministry of Finance in other cases.

## CORPORATE INCOME TAX

All legal entities operating in Poland are subject to corporate income tax. A legal entity with its registered seat in Poland is subject to tax in Poland on its worldwide income. Entities with a registered office abroad are taxed only on their income derived from Poland.

Taxable income comprises all income from all kinds of business activities. Generally, taxable profit is calculated on the basis of accounting rules. Normal expenses for business purposes are deductible, although certain expenses are specifically disallowed, and certain income is non-taxable. The profit of a representative office may be estimated on the basis of attributable turnover.

The general rate of corporate income tax is 40 per cent. Dividends received from another Polish company are subject to tax at a 20 per cent rate, which is withheld by the payer. Certain other specific profits are subject to different rates. Tax losses may be carried forward for a three year period and utilised in three equal instalments.

Tax holidays for companies with foreign participation are no longer available, however new tax incentives have been introduced which apply equally to foreign and domestic investors. Companies investing in regions of structural unemployment may write off their investment expenses as current costs in certain cases, and relief for investment costs is available for companies in all regions, provided certain profitability requirements are met. This relief is also available for some exporters irrespective of their profit levels, and for certain new investors.

Companies must submit a corporate income tax declaration and make prepayments of tax on a monthly basis.

## INDIVIDUAL INCOME TAX

Resident individuals are subject to personal income tax on their worldwide income (so called unlimited tax liability) from taxable sources. Non residents are taxed only on their Polish source income.

An individual is regarded as resident in Poland if he has a residence or customary place of abode in the country, or if he stays in Poland for six months or more in a given tax (calendar) year. This unlimited tax liability does not apply to foreign nationals who take up employment in corporations with foreign participation or branches and representative offices of foreign enterprises or banks. Such individuals are subject to Polish income tax only on their remuneration received for work performed in Poland, and on any other Polish source income (so called limited tax liability), regardless of whether they spend 183 days in Poland in a tax year.

In general, under Poland's double taxation treaties, a foreign employee of a foreign company seconded to work in Poland will not be liable to Polish income tax provided his presence does not exceed 183 days in any tax year, and if his remuneration is paid from outside Poland and is not borne by a permanent establishment or a fixed base which his employer has in Poland.

Income derived from the following sources is computed together and subject to tax at progressive rates of 21 per cent, 33 per cent and 45 per cent, after deduction of allowable expenses:

- income from business activities;
- income from scientific research, artistic, literary and publishing activities;
- lease and rental income;
- salaries and retirement pensions;
- income from assignment contracts.

Income from the sale of properties and dividend income is not aggregated with income from the above sources, but is taxed separately at different rates.

A fixed tax exists for certain crafts people, and with effect from 1 January 1994 a new 'flat' income tax has been introduced which applies to a large number of individual enterprises and to civil partnerships which, in the opinion of government officials, do not show real income if they are required to keep books of income and costs. The tax is calculated as a fixed percentage of gross revenue, which must be recorded in an evidence book. The new tax was introduced in order to ensure that a certain amount of income from small enterprises is included in the State budget.

## VAT AND EXCISE TAX

VAT, which together with excise tax was introduced in Poland on 5 July 1993, replaced turnover tax which previously existed. 1 January 1994 saw a significant change in the VAT law, but as the tax is still in its infancy a large number of areas remain uncertain.

In general, VAT covers domestic supplies of goods and services, and the importation and exportation of goods and services. Most entities engaged in business activities are required to register for VAT, provided their turnover reaches certain limits, and is not subject to a number of exceptions.

There are three VAT rates, a basic rate of 22 per cent, a preferential rate of 7 per cent and a zero rate which applies to exports and to certain specific goods such as medicines and newspapers. The right to a refund of VAT is limited, in general taxpayers have the right to deduct the amount of input tax from the amount of output tax, and surplus input VAT is carried forward. Certain goods and services are exempt from VAT such as low-processed foodstuffs, agricultural and forestry services, some municipal services, accommodation and communal services and financial and insurance services.

The Polish VAT system is broadly similar to the systems operating in the EU, with the main exception being the special treatment of the import of services, which is defined as services supplied within the Polish territory for which payments are made to a foreign party. The recipient of such services is required to pay VAT at 22 per cent on the amount of the payment abroad. This is treated as output VAT, with the result that it cannot be recovered by the Polish company. The irrecoverable VAT is however treated as a deductible cost of the payer for corporate income tax purposes.

Excise tax covers a typical range of excise goods. The tax is paid by manufacturers and importers of excise goods, and is discussed in detail in Chapter 20.

## SOCIAL INSURANCE CONTRIBUTIONS (ZUS)

All employers including foreign employers are required to make social security contributions on behalf of their employees, at a rate of 45 per cent of gross remuneration. In addition a further 3 per cent is payable to the unemployment fund, and 0.5 per cent to the warranty fund, giving an overall burden of 48.5 per cent. Contributions are also payable by individuals who carry out economic activities on their own account.

The remuneration of foreign nationals employed by a company registered in Poland is subject to ZUS, unless it is exempted under a bilateral social security agreement between Poland and the employee's country of origin. Board members' fees and remuneration received by a foreign national who is seconded from abroad by a foreign employer in work in Poland are not subject to ZUS contributions.

## REAL PROPERTY TAX

Real property tax is levied on all individuals or economic entities who are owners or freeholders of property. The rates are determined by each local authority, but must not exceed maximum amounts which are established by the Ministry of Finance. Typical rates range from Zl1331 per square metre for apartment buildings, to Zl50,211 per square metre for buildings used for business purposes. It appears from a recent government announcement that a new property tax may be introduced which will be dependent on the value of the property. The proposed tax has been strongly criticised by a number of groups.

## AGRICULTURAL TAX

All individuals and economic entities engaged in normal farming activities are subject to agricultural tax. The amount of tax is subject to a formula which takes into account the number of hectares farmed, and factors such as the class of cropland and the district in which the land is situated. A similar tax applies to forestry.

## STAMP DUTY

Certain administrative acts and legal processes are subject to stamp duty. Typical rates are 2 per cent for the transfer of movable property rights, 5 per cent for the transfer of immovable property rights and 2 per cent for the transfer of other property rights, including the granting of loans.

# 15

# Property

## Gerald Eve International

While knowledge of the basic legal rules relating to the acquisition and disposal of real property is essential to most foreign investors, it is only part of the arsenal required to complete real estate transactions successfully in Poland. Every bit as important is a proper understanding of the markets in which one wants to operate – both from a real estate and financing viewpoint, the psychology of the Polish people regarding property, the ever-changing turnover of personnel in organisations with which negotiations are undertaken, and the bureaucratic decision making processes inherent in most Polish companies and public sector institutions.

To assist foreign investors in operating in the Polish real estate markets, the Regulations section provides a working resumé of Polish real estate regulations. The second section provides a summary of the development of the principal property markets in Poland, and highlights key considerations for foreign investors.

## REGULATIONS

As elsewhere in Central Europe, Polish law has evolved from the Austro-German Civil Codes and the French Civil Code. The result is that there are many similarities between property law in Poland, the Czech Republic, Slovakia and Hungary.

The present legal framework for property is set out in:

- Polish Civil Code;
- Law on Land Management and Expropriation of Real Property of 1985 and 1990 (amended in 1992);
- Law on Perpetual Books (Land Registry) and Mortgage.

Foreign investors should also have regard to:

- Law on Companies with Foreign Shareholdings of 1991;

- Law on Acquisition of Real Estate by Foreign Persons of 1920.

These place certain restrictions on foreign investors when purchasing or leasing Polish real estate, requiring them to obtain appropriate permits in certain circumstances.

## Interests in land

*Ownership ('Wlasność')*

Ownership is the highest form of land tenure in Poland and is similar to the English freehold.

All land in Poland is owned by either the state, local authorities, co-operatives (groups of citizens voluntarily associated for social production) companies or private individuals.

*Perpetual usufruct ('Wieczyste Użytkowanie')*

A perpetual usufruct is similar to a long lease under English law. This interest was designed to enable the state to allow another person or body to use the land without having to give up ownership.

The term of this interest is for a minimum of 40 years and a maximum of 99 years. Unless specifically excluded, during the last 5 years the holder of a perpetual usufruct has the right to extend the term for a further 40 to 99 years.

Historically, the perpetual usufruct interest has been the main interest used by public sector institutions to promote the development of their landholdings. Consequently, the terms and conditions of usufruct interests often place an obligation on the owner to develop land in a certain way and within a certain time.

The holder of a perpetual usufruct has a relatively free hand in relation to its use, disposing of it by assignment or offering it as security for mortgage purposes. However, similar to a tenant under an English ground lease, breach of the terms of the usufruct could result in termination or enforcement action by the owner.

On granting of a usufruct interest, a premium is payable. Legislation stipulates that this cannot be higher than 25 per cent or lower than 15 per cent of the land's open market value, as determined by a certified Polish valuer. In addition, an annual ground rent of 0.3, 1 or 3 per cent of the open market value of the land is payable. Typically, if the land is to be developed for commercial reasons, a premium of 25 per cent is payable together with an annual ground rent of 3 per cent, if for residential use, the premium is 15 per cent and ground rent 1 per cent. There is provision for the appraised open market value of the land to be revised annually, although this often does not take place.

A distinction is made in Polish law between the owner of buildings and ownership of the land upon which the buildings have been erected, with the result that although the holder of a perpetual usufruct does not own the land, the holder can own the buildings.

*Occupational leases*

Polish law provides for two forms of short lease: lease (*'Najem'*) and rent (*'Dzierżawa'*). *Najem* were designed for situations where the lessee only requires an agreed occupational use of a particular premises. *Dzierżawa* were designed for use in connection with commercial land or land and buildings where the lessee requires to utilise the property for commercial benefit.

- *Najem*: maximum contractual term permitted is 10 years, after which the term will continue in perpetuity until terminated by either party on giving 3 months' notice. Main repair and insurance obligations and costs fall on the lessor, unless expressly provided for otherwise in the lease.

- *Dzierżawa*: maximum contractual term of 30 years, after which the term will continue in perpetuity until terminated by either party on giving 6 months' notice. The repair obligations and costs fall on the lessee, unless expressly stated otherwise.

In Polish law leases are regarded as personal rights and are consequently not assignable. Alienation is instead achieved through sub-letting, although where properties are sub-let, the original lessee remains liable to the lessor for any breaches of the head lease. Sub-letting is allowed by law if not forbidden by a respective clause in the lease agreement.

It should be noted that while the provisions of the Polish Civil Code set out a broad framework in respect of repairs, user, alterations etc for the above leases, this is fairly limited and often contrary to the commercial realities of transactions. As a result, it is usually necessary to undertake careful drafting in order to set out clearly the contractual obligations between lessor and lessee.

*Mortgages*

While the general concept of mortgages is well established in the Polish Civil Code, in practice their use has been relatively limited, although this position is now changing quite rapidly.

Mortgages represent registrable encumbrances over land and buildings. A notarial act is required in order for them to be binding. The entry in the Land Registry must stipulate the mortgage and amount secured.

It should be noted that establishing mortgages is quite expensive and enforcement costs can be between 10 to 15 per cent of the total claim, as possession and disposal of mortgaged property can only be effected through court proceedings.

### Land registry

There are two types of land register in Poland.

- Land registers (*'Księgi Wieczyste'*): these are now managed by the courts and describe the legal situation of registered property.

- Administrative registers ('*Ewidencja Gruntów*'): these are maintained by the local authorities and describe the occupier, area, borders, services, planning position, etc of a property.

Although land registers have existed in Poland for many centuries, the substantial disruptions experienced over the last 50 years have resulted in the destruction of many of these records. What records remain are maintained in script form with limited use of computer technology. The result is that there is a considerable backlog of unprocessed applications. Another failing of the system arises from the fact that many state-owned companies have resisted registering title to the land under their control in order to avoid paying land taxes. Consequently, proving clear title to a particular piece of land can often be difficult.

### Acquisition and leasing of land by foreigners

Foreigners are allowed to purchase real estate or perpetual usufruct interests, or commit such interests to the founding capital of a company on receipt of an appropriate permit from the minister of internal affairs.

Foreign investors will normally be granted such a permit provided two conditions are met:

- they are licensed to do business in Poland;
- it can be proven that it is necessary to purchase property for their business needs and that the property is to be acquired at an open market price.

Notification of whether or not permission is granted must be made by the ministry of internal affairs within two months of the foreign investor submitting the application. Strict guidelines are set out on the documentation to be provided in the application.

Where a foreign investor is planning to purchase property from a state legal entity or *gmina*, it will have to take part in a tender for the property first.

Where a foreign investor requires to lease land or buildings from the state or public company for a period of six months or longer, permission from the ministry of ownership change (ministry of privatisation) is also required.

### Building and development control

The process of acquiring planning permissions and construction permits for development is notoriously complex and politically charged, particularly where projects are high profile and project sponsors are foreign investors. Some of the problems arise from bureaucratic delays within the local authorities themselves, some through a lack of understanding of the system by foreign investors. One thing is clear: no foreign investor should attempt to obtain planning permissions and construction permits without the assistance of a Polish planning consultant.

Key steps in the approvals procedure include:

- Request for town planning information;
- Application for Location Recommendation;
- Application for a Decision on the Investment Location;
- Application for Approval of the Implementation Plan;
- Application for Construction Permit – this requires the applicant to provide evidence of their right in the site planned for development.

In addition to the above, it will be necessary to negotiate an investor agreement with the local authority in respect of infrastructure costs, ie connecting to services, etc. This will stipulate a sum of money to be paid by the investor to the local authority, and is based upon a percentage of the total anticipated investment costs. The exact percentage is negotiable, and will depend upon how badly the local authority wants to attract new business; for new build projects it can be as high as 15 per cent of the total anticipated investment costs.

As an indication of the likely bureaucratic delays faced by a potential foreign investor when obtaining appropriate permissions for a planned development, it should be noted that in order for the local authority to issue a Location Recommendation, it may be necessary to make representations to between 15 and 20 separate institutions or departments. While this may be relatively straightforward for an appropriately qualified Polish professional, foreign consultants will experience considerable difficulties interfacing directly with local authority decision making organisations.

## *Tax*

Principal real estate taxes are as follows:

- on purchase of property or a usufruct interest, stamp duty is payable at 5 per cent of the purchase price;
- on sale of the property, subject to certain exceptions, the seller must pay capital gains tax at a rate of 10 per cent of the sale price;
- local taxes are payable, and separately assessed in respect of both land and buildings;
- holders of usufruct interests must pay an annual fee of 0.3, 1 or 3 per cent of the value of the land.

### Restitution

The contentious issue of restitution – returning land and buildings to former owners where it was confiscated by the state after the war – has still to be resolved properly. While draft legislation has been drawn up, there are still many practical issues to be resolved that are likely to result in considerable further delays before any legislation can be passed on how to find an equitable, yet practical solution to outstanding land claims by pre-war owners.

### Expropriation

Polish law provides that land may only be expropriated under certain circumstances, for example reasons of national security, if it is in the public interest or where it is required for the construction of public amenities.

Where land is expropriated, full compensation equivalent to the property's open market value must be paid within 14 days from the date at which the compulsory purchase order becomes valid. Compulsory purchase orders and the level of compensation paid may be challenged in the courts.

## REAL ESTATE MATTERS

For those investors for whom real estate is their core business, there is undoubtedly considerable investment and development potential in the Polish real estate market. However, unlocking that potential is likely to prove elusive to foreign investors, unless they are prepared to commit significant time, energy and money into developing their knowledge of the market.

For those investors whose core business is not real estate, but who require a major real estate acquisition programme to support the activities of their core business, it is imperative that such organisations plan their real estate programme well in advance of any proposed market entry or expansion plans. Implementing real estate acquisition programmes in Poland is both a time-consuming and frustrating process, and has acted as a severe bottleneck on the planned expansion programmes of many multinational companies operating in Poland.

### Office markets

The office market in Poland offers a number of interesting investment opportunities, particularly in Warsaw which is presently experiencing significant demand for good standard office space, yet has very limited supply.

The Warsaw market is not easy for foreign investors: clouded ownership issues, confusing administrative divisions, a lack of constructive support from those in key decision making positions and the inexperience of new entrants on how the Polish market operates has resulted in many foreign investors incurring large upfront soft costs without making any real headway. This, coupled with a general nervousness among the financial community with regard to financing large speculative office schemes, has resulted in few project sponsors getting their schemes off the ground.

Where developers are successful, the potential returns can be very high. For example, the 8500 $m^2$ Warsaw Corporate Center was fully let within one year of completion on six to ten-year leases to institutional grade covenants. The headline rents vary between US$46 to US$50 per $m^2$ per month, with a 20 per cent add-on factor to reflect common areas and annual escalators of 3 per cent. This was for shell and core space where the sponsor was prepared to contribute US$200 per $m^2$ towards the tenants' fit-out costs.

While the achievable rents in Poland's second tier cities are substantially lower than for Warsaw, well-planned schemes should command rents of between US$25 and US$30 per $m^2$ per month. Where existing buildings are bought cheaply and refurbished to a good standard, profitable deals can be structured at these rental levels.

## *Retail markets*

The high street retail market is probably the most difficult real estate market for foreign investors to operate in. Limited supply of well-located stock and ineffectual bankruptcy laws often result in the better units being occupied without payment of rent or at very low rents by the old state-owned companies. Negotiations with existing tenants are extremely time consuming and in situations where tenants are in rental default, it is still difficult to get them removed.

Rents for Nowy Świat, probably Warsaw's premier retail street, are often as high as US$50 per $m^2$ per month, although a recent letting to Estee Lauder was rumoured to be based upon US$100 per $m^2$ per month. For other main retail streets in Warsaw, rents of between US$20 to US$30 per $m^2$ per month are being achieved. In the major second tier cities, rents for prime retail pitches are often in the region of US$25 to US$35 per $m^2$ per month. As with other emerging markets, actual rents achieved vary considerably due to the relative negotiating strength and sophistication of the lessor and lessee.

While the out-of-town retail market is relatively embryonic, there are a number of examples emerging of out-of-town retail schemes, such as Ikea and the Panorama Centre in Warsaw and the Euro Trans Park in Poznan.

## *Industrial markets*

Poland benefits from a significant amount of vacant industrial and distribution property, however little of its existing stock meets the requirements of modern day usage. Despite this, few developers have succeeded in getting warehousing schemes off the ground, although there are a number presently at the planning stage, particularly in Warsaw.

Rents for existing warehouse properties in Warsaw vary from US$3 to US$15 per $m^2$ per month dependent upon both quality and size. Most developers are budgeting between US$10 to US$15 per $m^2$ per month for well-located new industrial space in Warsaw. The exact rentals being sought depend upon size and the required percentage of ancillary office space.

Outside Warsaw, the rental patterns across the country vary between US$2 to US$6 per $m^2$ per month for existing industrial and warehouse stock; again, rents vary dependent upon the amount of space required and the quality of stock on offer. In certain cities, such as Poznań, rents as high as US$10 per $m^2$ per month have been achieved for good warehouse space.

To date few developer-driven schemes have emerged. Instead, most new industrial and distribution space has been owner occupier initiated.

## Hotel markets

Within Warsaw, the upper end of the hotel market is well catered for. The Marriott dominates the executive business market, the Bristol offers five star Forte elegance – perhaps three to five years ahead of its time – and the Victoria, Mercure, Holiday Inn and Sobieski complete the complement of the upper end of the market. There is, however, a strong need for more three star and budget hotels.

Outside of Warsaw, while a few hotels have been constructed in recent years, for example the Radisson in Szczecin, the Park in Poznań and the City Hotel in Bydgoszcz, most of Poland's second tier cities are in serious need of further hotels at three star level and below. The difficulties being encountered with the privatisation of Orbis – Poland's main state-owned chain with more than 50 hotels throughout Poland – and other state-owned hotel companies, has only served to exacerbate the problems caused by this shortage.

## Key considerations

Key considerations that need to be addressed by foreign investors wishing to enter the Polish real estate market include the following.

- **Upfront soft costs:** potential investors will require a deep pocket to defray the inevitable large upfront soft costs required to make things happen in the Polish real estate market.

- **Speed of financing:** ready access to own funds or backers with a short decision making process is essential in order to tie down positions on sites. While it may take a considerable time for the Polish side to reach a decision, once that decision is reached, foreign investors are expected to act quickly if they want the deal.

- **Costs of financing:** the cost of debt and the returns sought by institutional equity investors in the Polish market is high. It is essential to reflect this properly in the purchase price before committing oneself to a deal.

- **Title:** extreme care must be taken in this respect and a thorough review of title commissioned. Where it is possible to take out title insurance, this should also be undertaken, as in many cases it will not be possible for lawyers to guarantee clear title.

- **Planning:** as mentioned above, the planning system in Poland is notoriously complex. Never take planning for granted. This necessitates a thorough due diligence before purchase.

- **Services:** services laid on to a site or building must also be checked thoroughly. Most existing buildings have inadequate services to support, for example, conversion for modern day office use. The cost and time delays of laying on appropriate services to a particular building or site can easily turn a potentially good deal into a bad one.

- **Movement of goalposts:** when in negotiations with Polish landlords, foreign investors who want to succeed in the Polish market will have to learn to deal with the frustrations and embarrassment, particularly when reporting back to boards of directors at home, of dealing with continually shifting goalposts.

- **Bribes:** while bribes are not essential to make things happen in the Polish market, refusal to pay bribes, 'key money' or 'consultancy fees', will often result in costly time delays. This is most evident when dealing with planning permissions.

- **Domestic factor:** although Poland publicly craves for foreign investors, Polish landlords would much prefer to sell to domestic investors. There have been many instances where foreign interest in a particular property or development has been seen as a stamp of approval of the financial viability of the proposition. The transaction has then been moved sideways to a Polish investor or investment consortium.

For foreign investors, operating in the Polish real estate market is not easy and the mortality rate of projects is very high. Making the necessary contacts and learning how to cope with the system playing a straight bat takes considerable time. Despite this, the opportunities in the Polish market for foreign investors are significant. Most of Poland's existing commercial property stock requires to be either rebuilt or extensively refurbished. The monumental task this presents is more than domestic investment alone can handle.

# 16

# Employment Law

*Nabarro Nathanson*

## INTRODUCTION

The rules governing the relationship between the employer and the employee in Poland are contained in a number of laws. The primary law is the Labour Code of 1974, as amended and as supplemented by Decrees issued by the Minister of Labour and the Council of Ministers. There are other important laws such as those governing trade unions, redundancy, unemployment etc. A revised labour law has been drafted and is currently being considered by the parliament. The draft aims at eliminating differences between employees in the public and private sector of the economy and providing employment regulations more appropriate to a market economy. It also includes more protection for employees.

The provisions of the contract of employment and of any other act forming the contract of employment (such as an appointment, election or nomination) must comply with the Labour Code. Any provisions of contracts less favourable to the employee than those provided for in the Labour Code are deemed null and void, and are replaced by the appropriate provisions of the Labour Code.

The Labour Code applies not only to Polish employees and Polish employers (including companies incorporated in Poland with foreign participation), but also to Polish employees and foreign employers operating in Poland, unless the individuals involved are governed by special rules under international treaties.

## THE CONTRACT OF EMPLOYMENT

The contract of employment should be in writing; if for some reason the contract of employment has not been concluded in writing the employer is required to confirm the terms and the conditions of the contract to the employee as soon as possible. The practice in Poland is for short standard form contracts of employment, the mandatory provisions of law being incorporated by operation of law.

At minimum the contract should clearly specify:

- the parties involved;
- the kind of job to be performed;
- the date of commencement;
- the remuneration; and
- the employee's obligation to observe the disciplinary rules of the workplace.

The contract of employment may be concluded either for an indefinite period, for a definite period or for the performance of a particular task. Each of these types of contracts may be preceded by a contract for a probation period.

## TERMINATION OF CONTRACTS OF EMPLOYMENT

### *Periods of notice*

Either party may terminate at any time a contract concluded for a probationary period or indefinite period, subject to the requirement for termination to take place on a particular day – see below. The termination of a contract of employment takes effect after the lapse of the period of notice.

When a contract of employment is concluded for a definite period of longer than six months, the parties may provide for earlier termination of such a contract upon the giving of a two-week notice period. A contract concluded for a definite period shorter than six months may not be terminated by notice.

In other cases the notice period required to terminate a contract of employment concluded for an indefinite period depends on the total number of years worked by the employee, not only for the employer who is giving the notice but for all employers. The notice periods are as follows:

| | |
|---|---|
| Less than 1 year of work | 2 weeks (the notice must expire on a Saturday) |
| Over 1 year of work | 1 month (the notice must expire on the last day of a calendar month) |
| Over 10 years of work | 3 months (the notice shall expire on the last day of a calendar month). This period may be reduced in certain circumstances |

The total number of years worked by the employee includes periods of employment in former work, regardless of the way in which previous employments were terminated.

### *Termination procedure*

The procedure involves notification to an appropriate trade union of the intention to give notice of termination of a contract of employment concluded for an indefinite period.

The trade union has certain rights of objection but cannot prevent the termination once all the required procedures have been followed. It is important to note that the notice cannot be issued unless and until these procedural steps have been taken.

The employer is not required to follow this procedure in the case of liquidation or bankruptcy.

## RESTRICTIONS ON TERMINATION OF THE CONTRACT

A number of restrictions exist on the employer's ability to terminate a contract of employment, for example, if the employee is near the age of retirement or is on sick leave. In addition there are a number of categories of individuals who have special protection under the law and persons in these categories can only be dismissed, if at all, with the consent of certain bodies.

Persons benefiting from these protections may still be dismissed for fault. Restrictions on dismissal will cease to apply in the case of bankruptcy or liquidation of the employer.

## CONSEQUENCES OF UNJUSTIFIED AND UNLAWFUL TERMINATION UPON NOTICE

If the termination of a contract of employment for an indefinite period is unjustified or is contrary to the procedural provisions relating to termination of contracts of employment, the court – upon the demand of the employee – is empowered to nullify the notice of termination; if the contract has already been terminated, the court may require that the employee be reinstated in his or her job on the same conditions with the outstanding wages to be paid to the employee. Alternatively the court may order that compensation is paid.

If a contract concluded for a definite period or for the performance of a specific task has been wrongly terminated, the employee shall only be entitled to compensation.

## TERMINATION WITHOUT NOTICE

An employer may terminate a contract of employment without notice where the employee has committed certain faults. The employer cannot terminate the contract one month after becoming aware of the fault. There are a number of faults listed in the law, for example, the employee has seriously violated the basic duties of employees and especially where an employee has disturbed order at the workplace; been absent from work without providing a reason; arrived at work drunk or drink alcohol at work; abused social insurance or have abused other welfare benefits.

Termination may not take place if the employee has been absent for certain justifiable reasons. Termination may also not take place once the employee has returned to work after the reason for the absence has ceased.

Where termination is to take place without notice the manager of the enterprise must first notify the appropriate trade union of the proposed termination and the reasons. The trade union has three days in which to state its objections.

## CONSEQUENCES OF UNLAWFUL TERMINATION OF CONTRACTS OF EMPLOYMENT WITHOUT NOTICE

An employee who has had his or her contract of employment terminated without notice in violation of the provisions of the Labour Code shall be entitled to be reinstated on the same terms and conditions or to receive compensation. The reinstatement or compensation shall be decided by the Labour Court.

## REDUNDANCY

### General

A separate law exists dealing with the circumstances of redundancy, the Law of 28 December 1989. Redundancy is considered to be justifiable where an enterprise is reducing its labour force because of economic, organisational or technological reasons *and* within a three-month period the enterprise is intending to reduce either 10 per cent of its staff if the enterprise employs less than 1000 employees or at least 100 persons in the event that the enterprise employs over 1000 employees. Where the employer wishes to dismiss employees for economic, organisational or technological reasons, but is not able to satisfy the conditions relating to the percentage or number of employees just mentioned, then the same procedures apply as are set out above (with some modifications) and the employees are entitled to severance pay as set out below.

The provisions of this law also apply in the event of liquidation or bankruptcy.

## Procedure

At least 45 days before notices of termination are to be issued the manager of the enterprise must give written notification to the appropriate trade union or unions of the intention to issue the notices of termination. The trade union(s) must also be supplied with the reasons for termination and the number of employees to be dismissed.

Upon the receipt of the notification the trade union may request information regarding the economic and financial situation of the enterprise and details of future employment. The trade union is entitled to submit within 14 days proposals to reduce the number of terminations. Within seven days the manager of the enterprise must notify the staff of his or her views on these proposals.

Within 30 days from the notification to the trade union, the union and the manager of the enterprise should come to an agreement for the basis and the timing of the terminations. If there is more than one trade union in the enterprise, such agreement should be reached with all trade unions. If it is impossible to reach agreement, the basis for the redundancies would then be determined by the manager of the enterprise.

## Severance pay

An employee made redundant is entitled to severance pay equal to:

| | |
|---|---|
| 1 month's salary | if the employee has worked for less than 10 years |
| 2 months' salary | if the employee has worked for more than 10 years but less than 20 years |
| 3 months' salary | if the employee has worked 20 years or more |

# THE INDIVIDUAL'S RIGHTS AT THE WORKPLACE

The employer must issue work regulations detailing internal procedures in the workplace and determining the duties connected with the performance of the work. Such regulations are only required for an enterprise with a number of employees exceeding 50.

These internal regulations shall determine the basic duties of an employee and define what are to considered to be important violations of such duties. They should also set down the rules relating to time of work, the beginning and end of each shift, breaks, night shifts, the obligation and manner of confirmation by the employee of their arrival at work and the conditions regarding the presence of employees in the workplace after the end of normal working hours. The regulations should also deal with penalties for violation of disciplinary rules and contain provisions relating to safety at work.

In addition the regulations must set down the rules governing the following:

- the terms and place of payment of remuneration;
- provision of work to the employees;
- the organisation of the workplace;
- time schedules for meetings with the director of the enterprise;
- types of work not permitted to women and teenagers;
- provision of protective clothing.

It should be noted that the regulations cannot impose any duties on the employees greater than those contained in the law.

## TRADE UNIONS

The freedom to organise trade unions is one of the advantages of the new Law on Trade Unions of 23 May 1991. Under this law the minimum number of people able to establish a trade union organisation is ten. Unions are authorised to do the following:

- give opinions on matters concerning the interests of all the staff;
- supervise the conditions of safety in the workplace;
- determine the division of the social and housing fund;
- give opinions on matters relating to individual employees;
- issue opinions in the case of termination of contracts of employment concluded for indefinite periods – see above.

## EMPLOYMENT LAW RELATING TO DIRECTORS

A director of a company or enterprise is appointed by the appropriate body, such as the shareholders' meeting or the supervisory board. Such appointment may be for an indefinite time. An employment relationship may arise from the appointment.

A director who has been employed on the basis of an appointment may be dismissed at any time, immediately or on a specified date, by the body which appointed the director. Such a dismissal is deemed equivalent to the issue of a notice of termination of a contract of employment and the appropriate notice period must be observed. In cases where a contract of employment may be terminated without notice, a director can be dismissed, likewise without notice.

## WORKING HOURS AND TIME OFF

### *Working hours*

Except for certain professions, the basic rule is that working hours should not exceed 8 hours per day or 42 hours per week. In one month the total hours worked may not exceed the number resulting from the multiplication of eight hours by the number of working days. All other hours worked by an employee are considered overtime and require the payment of additional remuneration.

The total number of hours of overtime may not exceed 120 hours in a calendar year. Employees occupying 'independent' or executive posts may be required to work in excess of normal working hours without the right to additional remuneration.

Night time starts at 21.00 and ends at 07.00. For night work the employee is entitled to obtain increased remuneration at the rate of 200 per cent of the hourly rate.

### *Holidays*

An employee is entitled to holidays based on the number of years worked in their life, not just for the employer in question.

The periods of holidays are the following:

| | |
|---|---|
| 14 working days | after 1 year of work |
| 17 working days | after 3 years of work |
| 20 working days | after 6 years of work |
| 26 working days | after 10 years of work |

The period of employment on which the length of holidays depends includes periods of education, assuming that the employee has graduated from school or university.

## FOREIGN EMPLOYEES

The provisions of the Labour Code also apply to foreign employees employed in Poland by Polish companies or representative offices, as well as state-owned enterprises or other Polish economic entities. Foreign employees of diplomatic missions or certain international organisations will not be subject to Polish Labour Law.

Foreign employees must obtain a permit from the voivodship employment office. Such a permit is granted for specified period of time and it will state the kind of job to be performed or the position of the employee.

## SOCIAL SECURITY

The employer is obliged to pay a contribution to the social security fund in amount of 45 per cent of the gross amount of wages paid in the month. This Fund is operated by *Zakład Ubezpieczeń Społecznych*, commonly known as ZUS. Contributions are paid monthly. This fund is established for pension and health purposes.

The employer is also required to make a 3 per cent contribution to an unemployment fund and 0.5 per cent to a workers' compensation fund. This is also calculated on the gross wage bill and is paid monthly.

As a general rule the employer must also pay contributions to the social security fund on salaries paid to foreigners with contracts of employment with Polish entities. Certain countries have, however, entered into social security agreements with Poland which permit such payments to be exempted upon certain conditions.

# 17

# The Labour Market
*Jakubowski CTAD Ltd*

As Poland continues its economic reforms, albeit at a reduced pace, a labour force with tremendous potential is emerging, not least because of the characteristics of the Polish people. They are hard-working, resilient and adaptable. They are also relatively highly skilled and educated.

The Polish economy is recovering from a severe decline in output and GDP that followed the 'shock' economic reforms implemented in January 1990. Most of the state businesses were, by western methods of assessment, insolvent with no hope of a recovery in sales and net worth in the foreseeable future. The management and workforce had to face what appeared to be insurmountable challenges. Yet GDP grew by 1.5 per cent in 1992 and 4 per cent in 1993. The forecast for growth in 1994 is 4.3 per cent and is strongest in the industrial sector which grew by 6 per cent in 1993. The areas of highest growth were electronics, wood and paper, textile and the chemical industry. Credit for this growth is fundamentally due to the skills and determination of the labour force and ingenuity and enterprising spirit of management. Of course mistakes have been made but they have managed the process of change with remarkable tenacity.

Poland has a total population of 38.6 million and a labour force of 22 million: 8.3 per cent of the labour force are university graduates, and a further 62.5 per cent have achieved secondary and vocational school graduation. There is however a mis-match in the needs and availability of skills. This is due in part to the rationalisation of state-owned companies as they identify a surplus of productive skills in certain market sectors and skill categories. As companies take steps to adjust the ratio of people employed in a productive and non-productive capacity more labour comes on to the market. This is still the aftermath of the old system which promoted an illusion of full employment by having two people carry out a job that could be efficiently completed by one – a system in which businesses were production not profit oriented.

Considerable rationalisation has already taken place but the large state-owned companies continue to make vast losses due to over-manning and lack of investment. They are currently being underpinned by government in order to avert the devastating social consequences on the neighbouring communities. A good example is Nowa Huta in Krakow where the process of rationalisation has slowed down considerably.

The private sector has made great strides in developing staff with considerable management and organisational skills, and now has a good understanding of Western business practices, but there is still a large void between the need and supply of well-trained managers in large state-owned companies, hospitals, government and quasi-government departments.

There is a need for continuous learning and upskilling and to constantly re-address the issue of training. The Polish government has implemented a number of support and training programmes mainly for the unemployed and small businesses. It is common practice throughout the world that responsibility for training should be borne by the business community. In Poland there is no financial support from the state. While the Business Support Centres are providing a very valuable support service, these are funded on a pump priming basis through PHARE programmes and in the future funding will need to be committed by the Polish government. Both state-owned and private companies are currently expected to pay for training their workforce.

One of the profound effects of the transformation of the economic system in Poland is the level of unemployment. This has had to become a part of Polish life. The reality of surplus labour in a free market economy is generally understood if not totally accepted by Poles. In April 1994 unemployment stood at 15.7 per cent nationally, around 3.6 million people.

There are many obstacles to reform in the labour market but policy thinking is established and clear. The implementation focuses understandably on the issue of re-skilling and support for the unemployed. The organisational labour market infrastructure is being developed, providing stimulus and support for those who need to find employment or be re-skilled.

Mobility of labour is a huge challenge. In the previous system people had one type of qualification, one workplace, one residence for life. All these factors induce a lack of mobility in the labour market. A cultural change needs to take place which brings greater demands on the individual to take responsibility to develop themselves.

Poland is relatively stable economically, politically and financially. It also has a relatively stable industrial relations, particularly in view of the phenomenal changes that have been implemented during the past four years. Unions are tempered by the fear of unemployment. There is also a deeply rooted understanding by Poles that wealth creation and profit is a prerequisite to a company's successful development and growth, and in turn the country's prosperity. The illusion of full employment is a thing of the past. To put it in context, 20 years ago the UK had a much worse industrial relations record, dominated in the main by confrontation and strife.

In the last two years the privatisation process has slowed down considerably, particularly if compared to the challenging targets set by previous governments. This has provided a level of stability in the labour force which may have been difficult to maintain had the privatisation programme been continued at the same pace. Giving time to consolidate and become psychologically adjusted to the new methods and practices before moving to the next stage of rationalisation and restructure is not a bad thing. Progress is being made. In May 1994 the private sector accounted for 60 per cent of employment and 50 per cent of GDP. Small companies have been emerging rapidly. Since 1990 more than 1.7 million companies have been established by private individuals.

Remuneration of employees is through wages and salaries. Conditions of employment are contained in terms and conditions conforming to the Polish Labour Code. The average gross monthly salary in 1993 was US$225.80 with rates being somewhat higher in industry and communication, and lower in agriculture and forestry. Differentials are relatively narrow with a company director in the private sector earning an average US$892 and an assembly worker US$165. Wages in the state sector are 38 per cent lower on average than in the private sector.

Finding the right people in Poland is very much the same as in the UK. Job centres are administered by the Voivod Labour Office. These are run on a similar basis to the West with no charges being made. There are also a number of private employment agencies who are able to carry out the searching and selection process.

Poland has made remarkable progress during the past four years. The strategy in broad terms is clear. The development of this strategy is inextricably linked to the process of putting it into practice. When all is said and done it is people that make things happen. It is paramount therefore that the people in the labour market must be equipped with the skills and attitudes necessary to consolidate and continue the reforms.

*18*

# The Environment
## BMF International Ltd

## INTRODUCTION

To gain some understanding of environmental issues in Poland, its social and industrial history needs to be taken into account. Over the centuries Poles have always harboured strong feelings for their natural surroundings and unspoiled countryside. Even in 1934 Poland had already passed a law on the protection of nature. Unfortunately, the post-war Communist regime had other priorities when it initiated and encouraged a programme of heavy industrial development to try to rebuild the economy after the ravages of the Second World War. The regime's aim was production at all costs – without due regard for the environmental impact. With the majority of domestic research and technology institutions destroyed, and the 'Iron Curtain' rapidly coming down, the country had little alternative but to resort to the technology available within the Comecon block. Therefore, often inefficient and low technological production processes were put in place without any thought for the environmental damage which might occur. The accent was very clearly on manufacturing and not effluent treatment.

The legacy of such a policy is as follows.

- The poor management of municipal and industrial waste which often leads to toxic matter leaching into the local river ways and the water table.

- The lack of sewage treatment and discharge of effluent into rivers has resulted in 2.4 per cent being classified as drinkable and even 60 per cent being unfit for industrial purposes.

- High amounts of airborne pollution, especially through the poor control of the emission of sulphur and nitrogen oxides. For instance, the ancient city of Kraków has seen many of its monuments destroyed and it is estimated that substantial areas of forest have been damaged by the action of acid rain. Unfortunately this is not only a Polish problem as trans-boundary pollution is generated by all the former Eastern bloc countries.

- Inadequate land management following open cast mining.
- Food sources have been poisoned. For instance, the presence of a high concentration of heavy metals means that 10 per cent of fruits and vegetables, and over 20 per cent of milk is unfit for human consumption.

The decade of martial law severely restricted public reporting and information, and through this the social awareness of the damage not only being done to the environment itself, but also the hazardous and life-threatening conditions which had been generated for many communities, was limited. Once the political changes of 1989 had begun to set in, Poles were horrified to discover the extent of the damage – especially what had been caused by heavy industry, and were determined to take remedial action and 'clean up their act'. Laws to protect the environment and increase the size of fines were passed, and a 'List of 80' was published. This 'List of 80' is a register of the worst polluters in each voivodship, with the threat that the company would be shut down if it did not deal with its environmental problem by the end of 1995.

Unfortunately, economic reality has dictated that to date Polish industry has not had available the size of capital required to be able to put into motion a 'fast-track' clean-up campaign. That is not to say that Polish companies are unaware of the impact they are having on the environment, but with the limited resources at their disposal they are more prepared to pay fines and invest in restructuring their companies than for environmental projects. Their logic is simple – if the company fails, then the social impact will be far worse and harder to bear than putting up with their current environmental problem. Nevertheless, the authorities are getting far tougher in dealing with persistent offenders and prosecutions, and heavy fines and closures are becoming far more common place. This pressure, together with the awareness that without meeting or bettering international standard pollution levels by 1997 Poland will not be allowed into the EC, has spurred on many companies to strive to lower their emissions and discharges to an acceptable level.

## *The foreign investor*

As can be gleaned from the above, environmental issues are an area of business in Poland which can often generate problems if they are not dealt with with due care and attention.

For a foreign investor, environmental issues can have an impact within any of the main three areas of entering into, or doing business, in Poland:

- greenfield start-up;

- day-to-day operations;
- acquisition/merger.

It is evident that within all these business areas the environmental issue will play a different role and as such needs to be addressed separately.

*Greenfield site*

A permit from the Ministry of Environmental Protection, Natural Resources and Forestry (MEPNRF) will be required if the planned process will have any kind of impact on the environment.

The procedure is to apply to the MEPNRF, who in turn will appoint an independent expert, from a list of specialists already certified by the MEPNRF, to give a full evaluation of the planned project. A permit will be issued on the basis of a positive analysis by the MEPNRF of the specialist's report and only once the permit has been dispensed can the production facility be started up. This whole procedure can take six months.

Until recently the length of the process has not stopped investors breaking ground, as the permit granted by the MEPNRF only covers the production process itself, and usually not civil works and infrastructure. However, this loophole is in the process of being tightened – it is foreseen that the new Building Code will require an assessment of the technology the new facility will house even before any building permit is issued.

Note, the MEPNRF specialist may report that some aspects of the planned project will not conform favourably with current or even future environmental standards, and may even suggest how the process should be redesigned to accommodate these standards. In such a case the MEPNRF will insist that these problems are addressed and will only issue a permit once the process has been modified. An appeal process is in place if necessary.

An environmental impact assessment (EIA), is required for any investment which is deemed to be harmful, or in some aspects affects the environment or human health. The EIA is usually required during the question of localisation. The process of localisation (the siting of the investment) must be done locally and according to regional development plans defined in the Council of Ministers decree of 27 June 1985 on the Distribution of Investments and the Scope, Principles and Procedure of Assigning Localisation Thereof (a uniform text of the Act and all amendments was published as a Schedule to the Announcement by the Minister of Spatial Development and Construction of 16 February 1990 – *Journal of Polish Laws of 1990*, No 11, item 75).

MEPNRF and Chief Sanitary Inspector (CSI) approval are required for certain investments such as motorways and airports. The types of investments which require MEPNRF and CSI approval are defined in the Order of the MEPNRF of 23 April 1990 (Monitor Polski No 16, item 126). The voivodas also have the power to require the investor to perform an EIA during the procedure of localisation.

*Operational issues*

Permits are required from the local Voivoda's Office for Environmental Protection (UWOŚ) to cover the day-to-day running of the production process and would include such areas as:

- water uptake;
- water discharge;
- gas emissions;
- noise levels.

In the case of solid waste disposal, this permit is granted by the corresponding local authority.

The actual environmental performance of a production site is checked by inspectors from the voivoda's Inspectorate for Environmental Protection (WIOŚ). These inspectors can check at any time to see if the site is operating within permissible limits, and if it is not the inspectors have the power to prosecute, impose fines and even close down the facility, as well as setting the deadline by which the facility must be operating within the environmental standards. The permit issued by UWOŚ usually includes the level the company will be fined for exceeding a particular emission or discharge level. All fines collected in this manner go to the National Fund for the Protection of the Environment and Water Resources (NFOS) and are used to finance pro-environmental projects.

There is every indication that in the future permits will no longer be given to companies who use their own deep well water for industrial purposes, unless they are involved in agriculture, food processing or pharmaceuticals.

In addition, it is also highly advisable to become familiar with the local planning laws as these can impose even higher environmental standards, for instance, the proximity of a National Park.

*Acquisition*

One of the most important areas to check when making an acquisition are the past waste management practices in the widest sense, as once the site has been bought, the responsibility lies with the new owner. For example, does the factory have its own underground fuel tanks – are they integral, has there been any soil contamination in the past, could water supplies be put at risk from previous solid waste disposal practices?

The fundamental point is that the buyer should be wary, unless the issue has been covered in the sales contract. However, note that the government, be it represented by the Ministry of Privatisation (MoP), or the Ministry of Industry and Trade (MIT), will not accept unlimited environmental liabilities and each case is reviewed separately.

On the other hand, by the time the offers to tender for the target company have been sent out, the target company has already been questioned by the IEU as to the likelihood of environmental problems. (In order to address the issues of environmental liabilities in the capital privatisation process the MoP, in February 1993, formed an Inter-ministerial Environmental Unit (IEU)). If there is the suspicion of such a problem, then a Phase I environmental audit is usually commissioned from an independent auditor. This audit would cover such topics as past waste management practices, the technological process, the geology of the area etc, and would normally be accessible to any potential investor. If the results show that there could be a major cause for concern, then a Phase II audit would usually take place during the time of the negotiations. Apart from going in deeper into those areas already covered in the Phase I audit, Phase II would also include drilling test bore holes if water/waste contamination is suspected and would try to determine the extent of any current or potential environmental damage. It would also include recommendations as to what remedial actions need to be taken.

It is worth noting that there are currently no Polish soil standards for industrial properties, but recommendations should be in place by early 1995.

In conclusion, it is evident that the environment laws in Poland are becoming increasingly complex and under constant revision (the main environmental law of 31 January 1980 has been subject to numerous amendments – a uniform text of the Act was published as a Schedule to the Announcements by the MEPNRF of 21 March 1994 – *Journal of Polish Laws of 1994*, No 49, item 196), so it is strongly recommended that local legal advice is used and that the relevant local authorities are properly consulted.

# 19

# Utilities

## British Chamber of Commerce in Poland

## INTRODUCTION

Much of the infrastructure of Poland is in the process of being upgraded. The scope of activity in this respect includes both the provision of new systems and equipment, and the improvement of existing facilities to make them environmentally sound.

The finance required is being provided by a combination of state funds, private sector investment, and multilateral aid and loans. Three utilities sectors – energy, transport and telecommunications – are considered in this chapter as illustrations of the changes already in progress and those planned.

## ENERGY

Since 1990 the production of electricity has decreased in Poland. Nationwide consumption also went down but is now increasing. Industrial consumption in particular has continued to increase.

At present 97 per cent of Polish power comes from hard and brown coal (lignite). This has produced large quantities of dust and sulphur emissions. Targets for desulphurisation and improvement of air pollution have been set by the Ministry of Environment, and costs are estimated at between US$6 and 8 million.

The national demand for electricity can be satisfied from existing power plants and Poland has surplus capacity for the export of electricity. But as industrial needs increase, modernisation and renovation become more and more necessary. At present there are 55 power and heat-generation plants. The thermal power plants, of which there are 34 enterprises, supply over 50 per cent of the total electrical energy produced in Poland, the balance being generated through hydropower plants. Electricity is supplied through the Polish Power Grid Company, which is wholly owned by the State Treasury.

Electricity prices are fixed by the Government. Prices from 1990 to 1993 increased 60 per cent for industrial users and 300 per cent for residential users.

As from 1 June, 1994 prices for electricity have already gone up 10 per cent. A similar rise had taken place in February 1994.

Further increases are forecast with the aim of modernising power plants and improving the environmental aspects of the facilities. Heat prices and natural gas prices will also continue to rise. Overall energy prices are expected to increase at above the rate of inflation over the next three years. The VAT rate on energy is expected to stay at 7 per cent for the time being, despite earlier plans to increase it to 22 per cent. Prices, however, will continue to increase but keeping VAT at the lower rate will to some extent cushion the planned increases.

A small number of large power plants (three by 1993) and a number of district heating enterprises have been commercialised, that is, transformed into joint stock companies with a view to privatisation. No power plant has yet been privatised although the procedure is under way.

There are over 50 district heating enterprises; they use almost exclusively hard coal although there exists a conversion programme to oil or gas. The electric power sector is responsible for the production of heat.

Poland remains dependent on Russia for all of its gas imports and much of its oil. Alternatives are being considered, such as the supply of gas from the North Sea and Germany. There is also a project for the development of a new gas pipeline from the Russian Arctic through Poland to Germany. Meanwhile coal remains responsible for over 80 per cent of fuel used in industry.

British companies have won business in the modernisation of electricity generating plants, although opportunities in this area have been limited. Thomas Broadbent and Sons Ltd, for example, have installed large centrofuges at the Flue Gas Desulphurisation plant and the Belchatow power station. Any moves to privatise power stations are likely to arouse interest among British utilities.

## ROADS AND PORTS

The government has recently published a paper on Poland's transportation policy for public discussion. The paper deals with the issues related to the application of free market principles to transportation. The goal is to increase (a) trade, both within Poland itself and between its neighbours to the East and the West, (b) tourism and (c) foreign investment. Discussions are taking place with the World Bank with respect to the financing of projects in both road and railway construction.

The Polish railway system is one of the most developed in Central Europe but upgrading is still required. The time taken to transport goods is longer than in Western Europe – the main causes being speed limits, the condition of the tracks and the lack of an automated signalling system.

Poland currently has approximately 235,000 km of paved roads but only 600 km of this are dual carriageway. The amount of passenger cars is increasing 10 per cent a year and it is estimated that between the years 1990 and 2006 6.5 million more cars will appear on the Polish roads.

There are plans for three motorways in Poland: a north/south link from Gdańsk through Katowice to the Czech border (the A1 motorway); a west/east route from the German border through Poznań to Warsaw (the A2 motorway); and a further west/east route linking Germany through Wrocław, Kraków to Lvov (the A4 motorway). The costs for these projects are estimated at US$4.8 billion.

Discussions are taking place with a view to permitting toll roads and the operation of BOT schemes by private investors. However, legislation for providing a concession regime in this respect is still in draft form.

The Okęcie airport in Warsaw has already been modernised. Kraków and Poznań airports are currently being considered for modernisation.

British commercial activity in this sector has so far been largely limited to consultancy work, pending the opening of the motorway building programme to foreign interests. An exception is a substantial investment by the Dutch–British company, Gaspol, in a new LPG terminal in the Port of Gdańsk.

## TELECOMMUNICATIONS

The telecommunications sector is one which has already seen substantial improvement. Under the Communist system Poland was isolated from technological development, and the authorities had no interest in providing a modern telephone system. Following the fall of the previous system, one of the aims of the government was to avoid domination by imported equipment. Hence, in 1991 it ordered that telephone equipment sold to the public system be 50 per cent Polish. This led the way to the privatisation of the telephone equipment sector and the need for major foreign companies in the field to buy into existing state-owned companies.

During 1992 and 1993 all five major companies in the Polish telecommunications equipment supply sector were involved in privatisation, whereby the majority of their shares were sold to foreign strategic investors. These transactions ensure that there is access to modern technology for telecommunications equipment production and development.

The transactions in question were the following:

- the acquisition in November 1992 by AT&T of the USA of 80 per cent of the share capital of Telfa SA; the price paid was US$28 million;

- the acquisition in March 1993 by Alcatel Sesa of 80 per cent of the share capital of PZT SA and Teletra SA; the price paid was US$37 million;

- the acquisition in September 1993 by Siemens of Germany of 80 per cent of the share capital of ZWUT SA and Elwro SA. The price paid for both was US$38.3 million. Liabilities of US$30 million remained in the companies. Siemens agreed to invest US$57 million and to increase the share capital of the two companies by an amount of US$35 million. Siemens also provided employment guarantees for 100 per cent and 75 per cent respectively of the staff of the 2 companies for a period of 18 months.

The combined effect of the three transactions was as follows:

- 5600 jobs kept for 18 months;
- investment commitments of US$162 million over a six-year period (penalties are payable if the commitments are not met);
- capital increase commitments of US$70 million of cash;
- US$75 million earned by the state;
- debts of US$45 million assumed by the private sector.

There is now no longer a monopoly of telecommunications services in Poland. Telekomunikacja Polska Spółka Akcyjna is obviously the largest provider of such services but licences have been issued to private sector entities. Poland had the lowest number of telephone lines in Europe and therefore the market is extremely attractive for foreign companies. International telephone services remain the monopoly of Telekomunikacja Polska SA, which will continue to be a state-owned company for some time.

As at 1990 telephone penetration in Poland stood at 9 per cent. Since then over 1 million telephone lines have been added, raising the penetration rate to 11 per cent. The goal by the year 2000 is 25 per cent which is estimated to cost US$6–9 billion.

Private investment in the telecommunications sector is taking place. A joint venture is to be formed between Sprint, a US company, and RP Telekom, a Polish company, to develop a broad bank fibre optic network. Other Polish investors may become involved and the International Finance Corporation is also considering becoming an equity investor.

A cellular telephone system is now operating in Poland. It started in Warsaw but is being expanded to most major cities with a view of covering the whole country within five years.

The system is operated by Polska Telefonia Komórkowa Sp z oo, which is a joint venture between Telekomunikacja Polska SA (51 per cent), Ameritech (24.5 per cent) and France Telekom (24.5 per cent).

Satellite connection is also possible. Komertel was set up in Poland in 1992 and is a joint venture between Telekomunikacja Polska SA and AT&T Network Systems International. Other private telephone systems include a digital network established by Telbank SA, a joint venture between a number of Polish banks.

British telecommunication companies, including BT, have provided consultancy services.

*Part III*

# The Options for Western Business

# 20
# Customs and Excise
## Deloitte & Touche, Warsaw

The import of most goods into Poland is subject to customs duty, which is based on the customs value of the goods. In addition to customs duty, a new 6 per cent border tax introduced with effect from 1 January 1994, is imposed on all goods. This tax was effectively introduced together with VAT in July 1993, however up to the end of 1993 it was treated as an additional customs duty as the political situation in Poland meant that the introduction of a 'new' tax was not possible.

Imports may be made only in the name and the account of an entity which is registered or domiciled in Poland. In general a branch office or representative office of a foreign company may not import goods into Poland, unless the foreign company has signed an agreement with a local buyer, or if the goods are imported into a bonded warehouse which is administered by a Polish subject.

This chapter looks at the computation of customs duty and the modification of duty rates under various international agreements, then explains the administration of, and procedures for, customs clearance. There are also sections on customs exemptions, duty free zones and bonded warehouses, and finally excise tax.

## AMOUNT OF DUTY AND INTERNATIONAL AGREEMENTS

The basis of assessment for customs duty is the customs value of the goods, increased by the 6 per cent border tax; if the imported goods are subject to excise tax the basis of assessment is also increased by the amount of this tax. The customs value of the goods comprises the transaction value increased by any other costs up to the Polish border, such as transport and insurance, and commissions, dues and licence fees paid by the purchaser.

The conventional rates of customs duty range from 0 to 40 per cent, and these are applied to goods from countries with Most Favoured Nation status

(MFN). This includes goods from countries which are signatories to the General Agreement on Tariffs and Trade (GATT), to which Poland is a signatory. For goods imported from non GATT countries or other countries without MFN status, higher rates are applied.

Preferential rates apply to certain goods imported from the EU, from countries which are members of the European Free Trade Association (EFTA), from other members of the Central European Free Trade Association (CEFTA) to which Poland belongs, and from developing countries and less developed countries (in which the GDP is less than in Poland). Special rates apply to goods from Finland which has specific favourable status.

Poland has concluded far reaching agreements with the EU and EFTA which provide for the removal of customs duty on goods imported from the countries concerned over a period of time. A similar agreement exists with the other CEFTA nations; Hungary, Slovakia and the Czech Republic. Under the various agreements which were concluded in 1992, customs duties for certain groups of goods were abolished with immediate effect, and for other goods a timetable was set up for the reduction of rates to zero over a seven year period. This period is extended for goods in certain groups, such as textiles.

## ADMINISTRATION AND CUSTOMS PROCEDURE

Customs clearance generally takes place at the border, although some customs clearances have now been moved to major towns. An importer is obliged to complete a Single Administrative Document (SAD) at the point of clearance. The importer may declare the goods himself or use a customs agency, which would normally charge around PLZ 500,000 to PLZ 1,000,000 for a SAD document. There are also some fees for the customs clearance procedure and for the storage of the imported goods. The Polish customs tariff (PCN) consists of nine digit codes which are based on the harmonised European customs tariff (CN).

Customs clearance may be final or temporary. Final clearance is granted where it is intended that the goods will stay in the Polish territory. In this case the importer must pay all customs monies due at the time of clearance. Temporary clearance *may* be granted where it is intended that the goods will be re-exported, on submission by the importer of a financial guarantee to the customs office for the amount of customs duty, border tax and excise tax due. VAT remains payable, although it will generally be recoverable. Temporary customs clearance is usually available to companies leasing assets from abroad, although it cannot apply to passenger cars.

Customs duty and other taxes are payable by the importer within 7 days from the date when a decision given by the Customs Office evidenced on the SAD document is issued. The importer is obliged to pay the money directly to the bank account of the Customs Office if it exceeds Zl 20 million. Smaller amounts may be paid in cash.

## CUSTOMS EXEMPTIONS

Fixed assets which are imported as a contribution in kind by a foreign shareholder to a company's share capital are exempted from customs duty provided they are not sold within three years of the date of customs clearance. The assets are however subject to border tax, excise (if applicable) and VAT, although the latter is generally recoverable. The exemption applies to increases in existing share capital as well as to capital contributed to a new company.

## DUTY FREE ZONES AND BONDED WAREHOUSES

Duty free zones and customs warehouses may be set up within the Polish customs territory.

According to the wording of the customs law, a duty free zone is a separate and uninhabited part of the customs territory of Poland, regarded as foreign territory, where Polish, foreign or multinational enterprises may carry on economic activity, with the exception of retail trade.

The duty free zones currently existing in Poland are at Giliwice, Terespol and Sokolowka. There is also a special duty free zone at Warsaw airport, 'Okęcie', established to run duty free retail trade. A number of other zones were originally proposed by the customs law, however these have subsequently been cancelled. The trade in goods between duty-free zones and abroad is free from volume and value quotas, licences and payments due to customs. Business activity conducted in a Duty Free Zone is treated for customs purposes as if it were conducted outside the Polish territory ie no customs duty is payable on goods imported into the zones. In addition, the sale of goods located within a duty free zone is not subject to VAT or excise tax.

A bonded warehouse is a separate part of the customs territory of Poland, regarded as foreign territory, where Polish economic subjects, including the Polish subsidiaries of foreign enterprises, may store and deposit goods and also consign and prepare them for sale. Goods may be deposited in a bonded warehouse for up to twelve months, subject to financial guarantee, and this time limit may be extended in certain circumstances.

## EXCISE TAX

Excise tax was introduced in Poland with effect from 5 July 1994. Maximum rates for the tax are provided by the Act on Goods and Services Tax and

Excise Tax of 8 January 1993, however the exact rates which apply are set by ordinances and orders of the Minister of Finance. The tax is payable by importers and manufacturers of excise goods. It is not payable on the export of goods.

Excise tax applies to certain 'luxury' goods such as tobacco products, fuel, beers and spirits, wines, personal cars, yachts and hi-fi equipment, and to some traditional goods such as salt, matches and playing cards.

The rates of the tax are in the region of 5 to 25 per cent of the sales price for manufactures, and 7 to 100 per cent of the customs value increased by the amount of customs duty and border tax for importers. In the latter case the basic rate of customs duty is taken as the basis of calculation, even if a preferential rate of duty applies in practice or if the goods are part of a duty free quota. In certain cases excise may be stated as an amount per item. The tax is not recoverable, unless the goods are re-exported.

# 21

# Agencies, Distributorships and Franchises

*Nabarro Nathanson*

## INTRODUCTION

As an alternative to establishing a company to handle sales and marketing in Poland, a foreign company may appoint an agent or distributor nationwide or by region. Franchising is yet another way of doing business but this will usually require some kind of presence of the foreign company to monitor and control the franchised business.

## AGENCIES AND DISTRIBUTORSHIPS

There is no law specifically governing the relationship between a foreign parent company, be it a manufacturer or distributor itself, and an agent or distributor in Poland. In the past agents and distributors were often state enterprises, but now due to the rapid growth of the private sector in foreign trade there are many private companies who act in this manner.

Agreements governing agency and distributorship arrangements with foreign companies may be subject to Polish law or a foreign law. It would be advisable before choosing a foreign law on the grounds of neutrality to examine what protection or benefits are granted by that law upon termination to agents or distributors. They may be greater than those provided under Polish law, particularly in the case of certain European jurisdictions. In any case the agreement should provide for arbitration in the event of a dispute. Arbitration can take place in an international forum such as the International Chamber of Commerce or under the rules of the United Nations Committee on International Trade Law (UNCITRAL). Alternatively it may take place under the auspices of the Court of Arbitration at the Polish Economic Chamber based in Warsaw.

Since Poland is a member state of the New York Convention on the

Recognition and Enforcement of Foreign Arbitral Awards a foreign arbitration award will be enforced in Poland whereas a foreign judgment may not always be enforced.

There are no registration or filing requirements for agency or distributorship agreements.

## FRANCHISING

Franchising operations in Poland have increased dramatically over the last two or three years. Many of these are in the fast-food sector such as McDonalds, Pizza Hut and Burger King. Other franchises include the clothing sector and car rental. Petrol stations franchises are also being considered.

As with agency and distributorship arrangements there is no law on franchising. Existing legislation does not prevent or impede franchising. One of the most important laws relevant to franchises is intellectual property. It is essential that full protection is available to the trade name, the trade mark, the logo and anything else that goes up to make the image of the franchised product or service. In this respect see Chapter 24.

Another area of legal significance is the law on real estate. It is important that the franchisee is able to obtain adequate and speedy title to the property in question. There remain some problems in this respect both in connection with obtaining clear title and reprivatisation claims. The latter issue is yet to be resolved by legislation.

The advantages of franchising have been summarised in the publication of the United Nations Economic Commission for Europe entitled *East–West Joint Ventures* (issue no 3, autumn 1993). Some of these are set out below.

From the point of view of the Western company:

- franchising offers the possibility to expand sales and brand recognition at a low cost;
- it prevents risky investments in unknown markets;
- it does not need large investment such as that needed for a joint venture;
- it saves time, particularly when comparing with the lengthy procedures for setting up a joint venture;
- it provides a testing ground for marketing a firm's products or services, in relation to its future strategy;
- it could serve as a pilot operation for experimenting packaging or advertising, and adapting products to specific markets;
- it allows the control of the quality and marketing of products and services.

For the domestic partner, franchising advantages are:

- to start one's own business with the financial, marketing, advertising and other types of support of reliable Western partners;
- to obtain a stable market share of their own business through selling products of well-known brand;
- to ensure a permanent supply of goods of high quality with servicing guarantees;
- to learn Western methods of selling, servicing and managing from the franchisor;
- to benefit from the advertisements paid for by the franchisor;
- to establish relations with Western companies reluctant to enter into joint venture agreements, and thus provide the basis for expanding co-operation;
- to increase their own competitive edge over local competitors in the volatile environment of the transition process.

# Marketing

## Saatchi & Saatchi Advertising Poland

### INTRODUCTION

Until relatively recently Poland was a *planned* economy. Under this economic system there was no real necessity for marketing in its western sense. Production and distribution were determined centrally by the State and consequently the focus of enterprises was in predicting and fulfilling their set production schedules. Consumers and sales were low priority – in some cases planning even went to the extent of telling the consumer how much to consume.

Poland has now embraced the market economy. Progress is being made towards developing a marketing led consumer focused business orientation. The need for such a focus is increasingly recognised. All the main international advertising agencies are now in Poland, and for the success in Poland of consumer goods, advertising is now of fundamental importance. Polish businesses have quickly realised that, in order to compete with the influx of competitive brands from the west, they must become effective marketers.

The complete reorientation of a management approach is not easy, and for those older managers of state enterprises the learning curve is steep. However the number of Polish entrepreneurs and private sector managers has grown quickly since 1990. They are hungry for knowledge and are seeking to assimilate the best practices of western companies establishing themselves in Poland. The major western businesses here – such as Masterfoods, PepsiCo, Procter & Gamble – play an important educational role, and their business practices are closely studied. Over the past few years they have helped mould thinking with respect to best business practice and may even be helping erode some of the more traditional bureaucratic obstacles to change.

Access to good quality information is essential to a company's effective operation in a market economy. To meet this need market research companies are being established in big numbers. Some operate to western standards, but many do not have sufficiently experienced people to provide the type of support that major western companies would take for granted in their home markets. In addition the only statistical information available until recently was that gathered for government purposes. However this is changing in response to demand for market relevant information.

The present market situation in Poland is characteristic of an economy in transition. In many areas of the economy state control is still in evidence. This is most evident in areas essential to the country's economy such as energy, agriculture and transportation. On the other hand more and more product areas – cosmetics, clothes, household goods, audio and video equipment, cars – are being increasingly influenced by the workings of the free market.

## POLISH CONSUMER MARKETS

After many years of acute and persistent shortages, 1990 brought widespread stability to consumer markets. It came about as a result of a sharp drop in demand – the financial resources of the population decreased, in real terms, in December 1989. At present, supply of basic food and other raw materials or products is quite good. The estimated figures for 1993 indicate that US$15.9m was spent on the import of consumer goods.

It is estimated that 25 per cent of the Polish population lives on or below minimum subsistence level. A middle class 'western' standard of living is enjoyed by probably no more than 10 to 20 per cent of the population. Average household income per month for state enterprise workers is about US$250. However, these figures can be misleading. For example it is estimated that over 50 per cent of the population has a secondary source of income and that this boosts the national average income level by at least 25 per cent. In addition, according to official figures, Poles have in the region of US$10billion in zloty and foreign currency accounts. In any case, care should be taken in quoting averages in rapidly changing economic circumstances. Some jobs in Poland now pay six figure annual dollar salaries while others have, in relative terms, declined. Practically all goods found in the West are available in Poland. Electrical machinery (34.5 per cent), chemicals (17.8 per cent), and fuels and power (13 per cent) accounted for the highest percentages of imports in 1993. In the electrical and machine product group the most frequently imported products are colour televisions and computers. In the food category the greatest share of imports are for coffee, confectionery and citrus fruits. In 1990, 30 per cent of all cigarettes were imported. This figure has dropped below 10 per cent in 1993, as the number of local producers has exploded (currently there are more than eighty cigarette brands on the market).

Cosmetics, detergents, and personal hygiene articles account for the largest share in chemical industry imports, 40 per cent of clothes are imported and this accounts for 10 per cent of total imports. To give some comparison of prices, Tables 22.1 and 22.2 show the approximate costs of consumer items.

**Table 22.1** Consumer item costs

| Item | US$ |
| --- | --- |
| Packet of Marlboro cigarettes | 1.15 |
| Packet of locally produced cigarettes | 0.43 |
| One kilo of average quality sausage | 3.64 |
| One litre of petrol | 0.54 |
| Colour TV (locally produced) | 320.00 |
| Colour TV (imported brand) | 500.00 |
| Jar of jam | 0.68 |
| Imported car (Renault Clio, basic model) | 11200.00 |

**Table 22.2** Average income disposal

| Item | Approx % |
| --- | --- |
| Food (excluding alcoholic beverages) | 43 |
| Rent | 10 |
| Household goods | 14 |
| Consumer goods | 15 |
| (alcohol) | (9) |
| Clothes | 10 |
| Transportation | 8 |

It is interesting to note, that there has been a rise in the number of foreign companies producing consumer goods in Poland (ie Masterfoods, Procter & Gamble, Levi's, AT&T). By producing locally, these companies take advantage of lower labour costs, avoid high import duties, and demonstrate their long term commitment to Poland. In some areas (eg electrical goods) the number of Polish producers is in decline in the face of better quality and, in some cases, lower priced imported brands. This applies particularly to audio-visual equipment where such companies as Sony, Sanyo, Philips, Hitachi, Samsung compete for the Polish consumer among themselves as Polish producers have been squeezed out. Such products are usually imported by specialised distributors who provide guarantees and authorise after sales service. This form of after sales support is really a new option open to the Polish consumer.

# DISTRIBUTION

For forty years the distribution system in Poland was centrally planned and centrally managed. With the advent of the market economy this centralised distribution system disintegrated quickly. In addition, distribution retailing was also centrally controlled. The private retail business was really little more than street traders. In 1989 only 6 per cent of total retail sales was private sector.

As a result of the transition towards a free-market economy the national distribution and retail systems are undergoing enormous change. Much of the current distribution and retail structure can only be thought of as providing short-term solutions until sounder structures develop. From 1990 to 1993 only small shops and warehouses have fundamentally changed through privatisation. Indeed in 1993 the number of private retail outlets had increased to over 300,000. Large retail networks and wholesalers will also have to undergo the privatisation process. The elimination of the old monopolies from the distribution structure has forced trading companies, and in some cases the manufacturers themselves, to assume the traditional role of wholesalers. Currently, one of the greatest obstacles facing effective distribution is the lack of modern, functional organisations having a network of nationwide storage points, transportation fleets, information technology based stock control systems, and adequate warehouses. Wholesaling in the past has been totally ineffective by western marketers' standards. Recently, however, a small number of successful distribution networks have been established. These are serving as pioneers for others who will need to follow for the still far from satisfactory distribution situation to be adequately improved.

There are, however, examples of successful retailing and distribution. For example IKEA is successfully implementing its tested formula of manufacturing, wholesaling, and retailing in Poland. PepsiCo provides an example of a fully operating and successful distribution system. PepsiCo have put agreements into place which provide them with a franchise bottling and distribution network throughout Poland. This network will be managed from PepsiCo's Sales and Distribution Centre in Katowice, is supported by DSD (Direct System Distribution), and has a transport fleet which will service 13,000 retail outlets in its first year.

Over the last few years there has been a considerable improvement in the performance standard of retail outlets. Displays, service, and choice are all getting better. The siting of shops has become more regular, especially in residential areas of large towns where retail outlets had previously been sparse to non-existent. To a large extent the retail trade still lacks specialisation, (everyone sells everything) but this is also changing as retailers learn that it is much better for them and their customers to do some things well rather than a lot of things badly.

Many smaller shops prefer to sell mainly imported products as this ensures quicker turnover. For all practical purposes, a planned distribution system or policy does not exist and there is as yet no sensible grouping or segmentation of product categories at any stage in the distribution chain. Foreign trade companies eager to extend their ranges and diversify into new areas are duplicating imports instead of filling gaps in the market. This means that retailers are selling identical, imported goods which results in price wars and the lowering of margins. Many western companies recognised this weakness early on in 1990, and serious efforts are already underway to provide distribution systems to meet the needs of the free commercial market of the future.

## PRODUCT POSITIONING

The process of launching new or established products and creating their brand image is becoming more and more similar to western standards and practice. Due to an considerable increase in competition between goods in the market place, producers have begun to realise the importance of advertising and promotion. Producers are investing in consumer research to pinpoint how to position their brands in the Polish market. Advertising, marketing and communications specialists are used to developing and implementing marketing campaigns. Communications support materials – folders, brochures, POS materials, calendars – quickly become more sophisticated as the facilities for producing these become more advanced. Initially advertising was primarily concerned with communicating basic product information whereas now, in the face of much more intensive competition, there is a greater focus on effectively communicating brand images.

One challenge facing companies bringing their international brand and advertising campaigns to Poland, is that of being sufficiently sensitive to a culture and to consumers for whom the market economy, brands, and advertising are relatively new phenomena. There have been some marketing disasters attributable solely to the fact that insufficient thought was given to the suitability of an advertising campaign, developed for another market, for use in Poland. In these instances the advertising is just translated literally, without sensitivity to local consumers needs or understanding, has been misleading or misunderstood, and consequently been negative in effect. The challenge to advertising agencies is to provide the right mix of international expertise and local insight.

In Poland there were two traditional views about advertising. The first was that if a company, service, or brand advertised it would be noticed and that this would happen almost regardless of advertising content, because of the relatively small volume of advertising. The second view was that advertising a good product was unnecessary because, being a good product, it would sell anyway. These traditional views no longer hold in Poland. They have disappeared because the rapidly increased choice available, and the fierce competition which this choice has brought with it, have made such views clearly redundant.

The younger generation, many of whom have access to satellite television, enjoy watching western commercials and still tend to assume that western brands are of a higher quality than their Polish counterparts.

However, in recent years, these consumers are learning to become much more discriminating and general assumptions about the quality standards of all western products no longer hold. This is partly a function of the many advertising campaigns that have set themselves the task of highlighting differences, and partly a function of consumers experiencing the different quality standards of different western products.

## ADVERTISING

Advertising existed in Poland long before the market economy arrived, but not in a form modern marketers would recognise. Under the communists it was used as a propaganda tool. It was not very effective because it took the form of memos to the public of which the public were rightly sceptical. To a degree that sceptism still exists. Hence the worst thing an advertiser can do is overpromise; a product which overpromises will not be given a second chance.

Consumer choice is a market economy feeds on information. In meeting these new demands advertising is seen to play a crucial role. Polish manufacturers, in the face of declining market share and growing competition from imported products have quickly understood the role that advertising can play in their businesses.

As late as 1992 there was still just a handful of international agencies in the country, but by 1994 all the major agency networks had opened offices in Warsaw. Of course, as might be expected with any newly developing business, the standard of performance of these agencies varies considerably. In addition to the international advertising agencies there are numerous local agencies. Many of these agencies, which are generally small, have been formed by ex-employees of advertising departments of former state owned concern enterprises.

The pattern of advertising expenditure is changing dramatically. With big advertisers of nationally distributed products coming to the fore, more and more advertising spend is on television. The breakdown of advertising expenditures in 1989, 1991 and 1993 is as follows:

**Table 22.3** *Advertising expenditure by medium*

|         | 1989 | 1991 | 1993 |
|---------|------|------|------|
|         | (%)  | (%)  | (%)  |
| Press   | 51   | 42   | 32   |
| TV      | 18   | 33   | 56   |
| Radio   | 13   | 13   | 9    |
| Outdoor | 18   | 12   | 3    |
| **Total** | 100 | 100 | 100 |

The amount being spent on advertising is also changing. It is estimated that total advertising spend in 1993 was US$300 million. It is reckoned that this represents an increase of 100 per cent on the 1991 figure which itself represents an increase of 100 per cent on the 1989 figure.

The Polish population is big and it is broadly spread over a large geographic area. Therefore direct marketing has considerable benefits in theory, and some companies are making an effort to provide direct marketing services. However, because of the continuing inadequacies of the Polish postal services (lack of punctuality and insufficient infrastructure) and the relative unavailability of any commercially useful and valid lists, direct marketing is still struggling to get off the ground.

Transport advertising and roadside posters is now available in almost all major cities in Poland. The transport advertising concessions have been granted by the local authorities to a number of different contractors.

# MEDIA

The Polish media market is beginning to mature and now has most of the attributes of western markets. Some structural changes are still expected in the broadcast media, and new media are still appearing with great rapidity, but in general the types of options available to the English, German, or American advertiser are now possible in Poland. The role of the state has diminished, but is still important, as it controls the two principal national television channels and two of the four most important national radio stations. Legislation governing advertising is in transition but the tendency is to move towards EC norms.

## *Television*

97 per cent of households (12 million+) have a television of which over 80 per cent are colour televisions (in 1991 the colour television figure was 47 per cent). State television (PTV) has had a monopoly on licensed broadcasting with two national stations, Channels 1 and 2 and five local stations with limited broadcasting hours in peak time. However Polonia 1 has been broadcasting without a licence in twelve of the largest cities.

Recently licences to private stations have been awarded, notably to Polsat (a national licence), Kanal Plus (pay TV in several major cities), and two regional stations which each cover about a third of the country. Significantly Polonia 1 has not yet been awarded a licence but permits for local stations are yet to be announced.

However the Broadcasting Committee set up to award these licences has been subject to political pressures and its licence awards may be reviewed. It is expected that the Polsat national permit will be reconsidered. Currently there is much uncertainty about the outcome of these political pressures being applied and of the eventual structure of television advertising for 1995 and beyond.

An exponential increase in demand over the past four years has led to greatly increased levels of advertising on state television and also big cost increases. In 1991 there were 10,570 commercial spots broadcast on PTV, in 1993 the figure was 44,177, and that is despite zloty prices increasing by around 50 per cent every 6 months. Despite these increases television advertising in Poland is still relatively cheap with the cost of reaching audiences a tenth of the European per thousand viewer average. This makes advertising in Poland highly attractive.

Commercials are broadcast on state television from 8 am to closedown which is usually around midnight. Advertising can only appear before and after, but not during, programmes on state television. Advertising during programmes is possible, though with a cost premium, on private television stations.

Polish television viewing is very high. There is tradition of family viewing and little audience fragmentation except in major cities where Polsat and Polonia are available. The main edition of television news at 7:30 pm reaches 55 per cent of all adults. Channel 1 is a general family channel. Channel 2 is fairly similar but has some more cultural and regional programmes, it has slightly lower rating levels than Channel 1. The private stations rely on imported soaps, films, and series. They have to have a minimum level of Polish productions and this is confined to off-peak viewing hours. In keeping with the international accord for free access to information, there has been a marked relaxation of bureaucracy surrounding the installation of television satellite dishes. 11 per cent of households now have satellite dishes installed. Most new housing developments have a commercial dish built in for use by all residents. Audiences for international commercial satellite channels are now significant, for example: MTV (3 per cent daily coverage), RTL (2 per cent), Eurosport (2 per cent), Sat 1 (2 per cent), DSF Berlin (1 per cent), and PRO7 (1 per cent). 17 per cent of households have cable TV installed.

Without any doubt television is by far the most significant medium in shaping public opinion in Poland particularly for the middle and lower income groups who comprise the major share of the population.

## *Radio*

96 per cent of Polish families have at least one radio at home. One driver in every two has a car radio. 56 per cent of Poles tune in to a Polish station each day. PRT runs the four state-owned nationwide radio stations. Programme 1 is the most popular with 26 per cent daily listenership with a mainly housewife target audience. Programme III has 7 per cent concentrated among younger listeners. Programmes II and IV reach 3 per cent and 2 per cent respectively. State radio has also 16 local stations in

main cities with an adult housewife profile. Three private radio stations have been awarded national licences: Radio ZET, RMF, and Catholic Radio Maryja. There are also around 80 private local stations which have just received local licences, although most of these had been broadcasting for some time previously. These are of mixed quality but can be important media in some cities especially for a youth audience.

## Press

In January 1990 AGPOL, the state-run Foreign Trade Publicity and Publishing Enterprise, lost its monopoly on placing foreign advertising in the print media. AGPOL used to take foreign orders and place them with Prasa Ksiazka Ruch (RSW) – formerly owned by the Communist Party – who process domestic sales orders. From there they would be distributed among the twenty one publishing houses also run by RSW. The press market is now completely privatised with publications usually selling their own space although a few sales houses exist.

The choice and quality of the press market is increasing at a fast rate in all areas. Women's monthlies are dominated by strong Polish titles although both *Elle* and *Cosmopolitan* are preparing to launch. Among the monthlies the most popular is *Poradnik Domowy* with circulation of 2 million copies. This is a Polish women's magazine which has been a big success since it launched in 1990. Formerly strong Polish women's weeklies (eg *Kobieta i Zycie* with 200,000 copies and *Przyjaciolka* with 1,300,000) are now facing competition from German imports such as *Tina* (1,400,000) which is now the best selling title in the sector. Foreign investment has created a TV Guide market with the largest circulation going to free supplements in the regional press. Polish Television also publishes a television programme listings title called *Antena*. Specialist interest and trade markets still have enormous growth potential and new titles appear frequently.

The national press is relatively weak with only *Gazeta Wyborcza* as a mass market high circulation title with a circulation up to 800,000. *Rzeczpospolita*, (a business broadsheet) is read by top and middle managers with a circulation of 200,000. *Express Wieczorny* and *Super Ekspress* (both down-market newspapers) have circulation of about 500,000 and 100,000 respectively. However the real strength of the newspapers market is in regional press with many titles having circulation's up to 150,000.

Among the general news weeklies are *Polityka* with a circulation of 200,000 and Wprost with 350,000. Print quality in this area is low. Additionally there are numerous local daily newspapers which are very important in reaching regional markets and are often more popular than the national dailies. *Gazeta Bankowa* (weekly) with a 40,000 circulation and *Businessman* (monthly) with 60,000 are important titles for reaching business and management audiences.

## FAIRS, CONFERENCES AND MISSIONS

Trade fairs have been an important means of selling foreign goods to Poland. The most important is the Poznan International Trade Fair which is held annually, opens on the second Sunday of June, and lasts eight days. During the eight days about fifty countries will be represented. Foreign participants are usually organised on a national pavilion basis. The Poznan Fair Authorities also organise a series of specialised International fairs which take place in the spring and autumn. The areas covered include mining, energy, metallurgy, agricultural and medical equipment. In addition to Poznan there are many established and emerging fairs organised in Poland. For example there is the Warsaw Book Fair and the International Computer Exhibition. However dependence on trade fairs is diminishing as other channels of communication develop and provide alternative means of promotion.

Small exhibitions can also be effective and many companies organise such events. These usually take place in city hotels.

Another opportunity for businesses to market their products is by taking part in trade missions. Usually led by government ministers or prominent industrialists these receive a lot of attention in Poland. The CBI plans, as part of the Initiative Eastern Europe, such missions into Poland.

# 23

# Trade Finance

## *RZB-Austria*

With the rapid development of the Polish banking system, the British exporter seeking to trade with Poland has a widening range of options to enable them to offer trade finance to Polish importers. This chapter will explore some of these.

Although it is not a local legal requirement, Polish banks will usually look for cash collateral, before opening letters of credit, and exporters are often asked to seek ways of avoiding the necessity of opening a letter of credit and are under some pressure to trade on open account terms. It is not surprising that given the difficulty of finding alternative routes and the recent history of high levels of inflation – up to 30 per cent per month – which encouraged a psychology of making early payments, a relationship can often be commenced with the importer making payments in advance.

Unfortunately, the Polish financial sector has not developed a factoring capability, so that if payment in advance is not possible, the next level of sophistication is represented by the various collection procedures offered by banks. Typically, a bill of exchange with accompanying shipping documents is sent to the buyer's bank and the documents are released to the buyer against acceptance/payment of the bill.

Once a relationship has been established, it may well be possible to put some form of insurance in place. Following the privatisation of the short-term ECGD business, and its acquisition by NCM of Holland, there are two main private insurers (NCM and Trade Indemnity) providing cover for Poland, and ECGD has recently come on cover again for medium-term transactions.

## NCM

NCM have been providing cover for Poland since mid-1991, and can now claim to be fully experienced having paid their first claim at the end of 1993. Cover is short-term, ie typically 90 days and with a maximum of 180 days.

(The gap between the maximum of 180 days' cover offered by NCM, and the minimum of 2 years offered by ECGD is more apparent than real as sellers looking for more than 180-day terms will be looking to offer the subsided consensus rates available from ECGD for terms over 2 years.)

Small amounts – say £20–30,000 – can be covered on an open account where there is a track record (typically, these would be pharmaceuticals or speciality chemicals where goods are dispatched immediately on receipt of a faxed order). Larger amounts always require a letter of credit, probably from Bank Handlowy which currently covers 70/80 per cent of Polish import business or from one of the Western banks such as Raiffeisen Centrobank SA.

## TRADE INDEMNITY

Trade Indemnity is the main competitor to NCM for short-term business. The company's policy is to write whole turnover policies, so they are not looking to cover one-off exports to any particular markets. However, within the above limitation, they advise, at the time of writing, that they have plenty of capacity for new business.

## ECGD

ECGD completed a review of Poland in the first half of 1993 and came back on cover in July of that year. However, the cover is made available under ECGD's special support facility for countries like Poland which have recently rescheduled past due debts with the 'Paris Club'. The facility, which is know as 'DX Cover', limits cover to exports which have a beneficial impact on the country's foreign exchange earnings. This can be done by either enhancing the country's own export earning potential or, alternatively, through developing possibilities for import substitution. Cover for the import of luxury consumer products is definitely out.

The amount of cover is also limited so that individual transactions in excess of £2–3 million would most likely not be approved and the available capacity is on a 'first come, first served' basis.

The question of what support ECGD should seek as collateral was initially the cause of some heart searching. Their early requirement, when the country first came back on cover, of a ministry of finance guarantee in support of all facilities did not square with pressure from other sources for Poland to democratise/privatise as fast as possible. The situation has now been resolved, and ECGD will accept Bank Handlowy guarantees for 'substantial amounts', and Polish Development Bank or Export Development Bank guarantees for 'moderate amounts'.

Once the expense has been incurred of obtaining a bank guarantee, it could be argued that there is no further benefit in paying an additional insurance premium for ECGD support, as the transaction can be dealt with on an 'a forfait' basis (see below). However, this ignores the benefits to be obtained from accessing the fixed rate consensus financing – otherwise known as CIRR (commercial interest reference rate). In particular, it should be noted that it is possible to fix the rate even prior to obtaining a firm contract. Although this results in paying a 20 basis point surcharge on the rate, it still offers the exporter a valuable marketing tool – especially in a rising interest rate environment.

In the absence of ECGD support – eg where the goods have an excessive foreign content, or fall outside the 'DX' parameters – use may be made of the forfaiting market. This approach entails bills of exchange or promissory notes, guaranteed by a prime Polish bank, being sold 'without recourse' by the exporter to a bank. At the time of writing, there is a market for transactions with maturities out to five years with a Bank Handlowy guarantee and to three years with that of other prime banks. The paper is bought on a discount basis at a margin over the relevant LIBOR rate – current margins being in the order of 4 per cent per annum.

The question of leasing in Poland is somewhat problematic at present. The introduction of VAT in July 1993 has led to cross-border leasing becoming uneconomic, as VAT is chargeable on the leases but not reclaimable.

Finally, where all usual banking solutions fail, one should consider the possibility of counter-trade. With the zloty virtually convertible, this is of less interest than previously, but specialised counter-trade operations in Warsaw are able to handle the following:

- acting as fiduciary agents for cross-border transactions;
- performance of barter and parallel transactions;
- fulfilment of counter-trade obligations;
- buy-back obligations from delivered manufacturing equipment;
- switch and clearing transactions.

While there is less demand for this type of transaction today, the mechanisms are well understood, and there are a number of specialised institutions able to structure transactions and arrange the off-take of the products. FJ Elsner & Co in Vienna or EPALG in Warsaw are happy to offer advice on potential transactions (see Appendix 3 for contact details).

# 24

# Intellectual Property

*Nabarro Nathanson*

## INTRODUCTION

Poland has already taken important steps in modernising its intellectual property system and further draft laws are under preparation. Current laws include older statutes covering patents and trade marks (as amended), and a new law on copyright.

Poland has made international commitments to upgrade its intellectual property protection. For example, in the Association Agreement that Poland has signed with the EU, Poland has agreed to approximate its laws to those of the EU, including its laws on intellectual property.

## COPYRIGHT AND RELATED RIGHTS

Poland enacted the Copyright and Related Rights Law on 4 February 1994, effective as of 23 May 1994. This law substantially complies with the basic requirements of the EU Directives, particularly in the case of computer programmes, where the Polish law has practically assimilated the entire text of the EU Software Directive. On the international level, Poland is a party to the Berne Convention on Copyright Protection.

### The nature of copyright

Copyright extends to any manifestation of individual creative activity, set in any form, independent of its value, designation or manner of expression. The law differentiates between two types of author's rights. The first is personal copyright which protects the relation between the author and his or her work. This right is eternal and not capable of waiver or transfer. The second is proprietary copyright where, unless otherwise provided in the law, the author has the exclusive right to use the work and control it, and to receive remuneration for use of the work.

Subject to the exceptions provided in the law, proprietary copyright expires 50 years from the author's death; if the author is unknown or if a person other than the author owns the proprietary right, the period of 50 years runs from the first publication. Proprietary copyright is transferrable.

### Audiovisual works

The new law contains special provisions concerning audiovisual works. Proprietary copyright to an audiovisual work is held by the producer.

### Computer software

The new law provides protection for computer software. The protection extends to all forms of software, including design, production and documentation on how to use the software. Unless otherwise provided for in an employment agreement, proprietary rights to computer software created by an employee resulting from the performance of his or her duties are held by the employer.

### Protection of related rights

The Copyright Law acknowledges, for the first time, the protection of 'related' rights. Related rights include rights to artistic performances, rights to phonograms and videograms, and rights to broadcasts. These rights, however, are only given minimal levels of protection.

### Criminal liability

The new law introduces strict penalties for parties who infringe another party's rights. For example, a person who, without authorisation, distributes someone else's work, artistic performance, phonogram, videogram or broadcast in the original or a transformed version, may be imprisoned or fined. In some cases the court may order the forfeiture of all objects originating from the crime or used to commit it, even if they do not belong to the perpetrator.

## PATENTS

### Introduction

Patents are regulated in Poland under the Law on Inventive Activity of 19 October 1972, as amended. Although this law provides protection for inventions, the Polish patent law is widely regarded as in need of updating and Poland is considering a proposal for a comprehensive new patent law.

### International patent relations

Poland has been a member of the Paris Convention for the Protection of

Industrial Property since 10 November 1919; it has also signed the Stockholm Act and the Patent Co-operation Treaty.

Under the US–Poland Treaty, Poland has agreed to provide product as well as process protection for pharmaceuticals and chemical substances. In that Treaty Poland further assented to (a) 'provide a term of protection of 20 years from filing for patents in all areas of technology', (b) limit compulsory licences of patented technology and (c) provide patent protection for foodstuffs, pharmaceutical products and chemical products.

## Scope of coverage

Patent protection is accorded to any inventive 'solution of a technical character' that is new, non-obvious and capable of practical application. An invention is new if it was not made available to the public before the priority date of the application. There is no grace period under Polish patent law. An invention is made available to the public if it is published, publicly implemented or displayed at a public exhibition in such a way as to give an expert sufficient information for its application. An invention is non-obvious if it does not 'obviously result from the prior art'.

There are a number of statutory exclusions from patent protection. Scientific principles and discoveries, new plant varieties and animal breeds, and inventions whose exploitation would be contrary to law or public policy are not patentable. Processes for treating diseases in the fields of medicine, veterinary science and plant protection are not patentable. Foodstuffs, pharmaceutical products and chemical products are not patentable. However, the processes to produce these products are patentable.

Polish law provides for five types of patents: full; provisional; dependent; patents of addition; and secret. A full patent is granted by the patent office on the basis of a complete examination of the criteria discussed above. A provisional patent may be granted on the basis of an initial examination covering the application formalities, and a review of granted Polish patents and published applications. Dependent patents are issued where the exploitation of the invention requires use of a previously granted patent. The Patent Office grants patents of addition for improvements or additions to inventions which would not be patentable independently. Secret patents, which are not published, are granted for inventions of importance to national security of defence.

## Obtaining patent rights

Patent applications are filed with the Patent Office. The application includes a request for a patent and a description of the invention, and an abstract of the description and drawings as necessary. The application must state whether the applicant is seeking a provisional patent or a full patent.

Priority of patent claims is established on the basis of the filing date with the Patent Office. However, foreign applicants may claim international priority under the Paris Convention based on the date of first filing in a convention country, provided that the Polish application is filed within 12 months of the prior foreign application. Priority also may be claimed on the basis of the exhibition of the invention in Poland or abroad if the patent application is submitted within six months of the exhibition.

A patent confers upon the patentee the exclusive right to exploit the invention throughout Poland. Where an invention is made by more than one person working together, the patent belongs to all the inventors jointly. The scope of a particular patent is determined by the claims contained in the patent specification. A patent granted for a process of manufacture also covers products directly obtained from the process.

Polish law also protects prior users. Any person who has worked an invention in good faith within Poland or who has made substantial plans to use an invention in Poland, prior to the date of priority of the patent on that invention, has the right to continue to work the invention to the extent of the previous use without paying any fee.

### *Inventions created during employment*

If an invention is produced under an employment agreement providing for such invention, the employer is entitled to the patent. The employment agreement will govern compensation for the invention except where the contractual compensation is 'manifestly too low in comparison with the benefits' obtained by the employer. In such a case, the employee may claim additional compensation.

### *Duration*

The basic patent term of protection is 15 years from the date of filing. Provisional patents are granted for a five-year term. However, the owner of a provisional patent may apply to convert the provisional patent into a patent within four years of filing the initial application. The term of a transformed provisional patent is 15 years. A patent of addition expires when the underlying patent expires. The term of protection of a dependent patent is 15 years. Upon expiration of the independent patent, the dependent patent becomes an independent patent for the remainder of the 15-year term.

### *Compulsory licensing*

Under certain circumstances the Patent Office is authorised to grant a compulsory licence.

Within four years from the filing date of a patent application, or three years from patent grant, whichever is longer, the patentee must begin to exploit the invention in Poland 'on a scale appropriate to the needs of the national economy'. The use requirement can be satisfied by licensing the invention. The Patent Office may request information on the extent and nature of use, including explanations for non-use or inadequate use.

If a patent invention is being insufficiently worked, the Patent Office may solicit applications for compulsory licences. A person working an invention under a compulsory licence must pay appropriate royalty amounts to the patent-holder.

### Enforcing rights

A person whose patent has been infringed may demand the cessation of the infringement or the payment of damages. The injured party also may demand that the infringing party publish an explanatory statement. If the infringement is intentional, the infringer may be required to pay a penalty to the Central Technological Organisation to be used to encourage inventive activity.

## TRADE MARKS

### The law

The Law on Trade Marks of 1985, as amended, regulates the 'legal relations and procedure' governing the 'protection and use in economic activity of trade marks for goods and services in Poland'.

### International agreements

Poland is a member of a number of international agreements relating to trade marks including the Paris Convention for the Protection of Industrial Property, Stockholm Act, the Madrid Agreement concerning the International Registration of Marks, the Madrid Agreement for the Repression of False or Deceptive Indications of the Source of Origin and the Hague Act.

### Protection of foreign marks

Consistent with its international obligations, Poland accords national treatment to foreign natural and legal persons under Polish law. In addition, under a broad reciprocity provision, any foreign national may seek national treatment in Poland, if the national laws of the home jurisdiction afford Polish nationals the same rights.

### Scope of coverage

Protection is available under the Polish law for trade marks and service marks. Trade names are protected under the Polish Civil Code and the Unfair Competition Law.

Trade marks are broadly defined as 'any sign capable of distinguishing the goods or services of a given enterprise from similar goods or services of another enterprise'. 'Words, designs, ornaments, combinations of colours, plastic forms, melodies or other acoustic signals' and any combination of these elements are all eligible for protection.

Marks may be denied registration by the Patent Office if they are likely to mislead the public. If used in connection with the same goods, the following types of marks have the potential to mislead the public:

- marks that resemble registered marks of another enterprise;
- marks that are similar to well-known marks;
- marks that are similar to previously registered expired marks within three years of the lapse;
- marks that indicate a geographic location that is not in fact the source of the trade marked goods.

Owners of well-known marks are afforded protection for their marks even without registration or use in Poland. The only requirement is that the mark be well known in Poland. The Polish courts, for example, have protected the trade mark 'Wrangler' as a world-famous mark. The owner of a famous mark may:

- request the annulment of a registered mark which is so similar that it creates public confusion; or
- prohibit its use by third parties.

## *Registration of trade marks*

Trade mark rights are obtained through registration. Applications for the registration of trade marks are filed with the Polish Patent Office.

Priority of registration is granted to the first applicant, based on the date of filing. A foreign applicant may establish an international priority under the Paris Convention by filing an application in Poland within six months of the date of a home application, or within six months of the date of public display of the goods bearing the trade mark in Poland or in another Paris Convention member country.

## *Duration*

The trade mark registration lasts for ten years from the date of filing of the application, renewable for further ten-year periods. The request for renewal must be filed not earlier than one year before expiration. The trade mark owner must establish three years of consecutive use of the mark in connection with the goods or services for which renewal is sought.

## *Assignment and licensing*

Trade mark rights may be assigned. The contract of assignment must be in writing, bear a certified date and be recorded in the Trade Mark Register.

A trade mark owner may license another with the right to use the mark for goods or services covered by the registration. The licence agreement, which should be in writing, authorises the licensee to use the mark 'in the same way as the owner of the rights', unless the agreement specifically states otherwise. To enable the licensee to act against third parties violating the trade mark, the licence must be filed in the Trade Mark Register.

### *Cancellation*

A trade mark registration may be cancelled for any of the following reasons:

- expiration of the term of protection without renewal;
- abandonment;
- non-use;
- loss of distinctiveness; and
- termination of the economic activity upon which the trade mark registration was based.

After five years, trade mark rights are no longer subject to cancellation, unless the owner obtained the registration in bad faith.

### *Enforcement*

The trade mark owner may apply to the court for the following protection:

- an injunction to cease the infringing activity;
- damages and surrender of unlawful profits;
- seizure of the infringing goods; and
- an order requiring the removal of the infringing mark from products already in the market and from advertising with that mark.

Infringement actions are subject to a three-year period of limitation. A recent amendment to the trade mark law has strengthened the protection available by providing for criminal sanctions for infringement.

## INDUSTRIAL DESIGNS, UTILITY MODELS AND SEMICONDUCTORS

### *Industrial designs*

Poland provides protection for industrial designs. Design protection covers the aesthetic elements of commercial products, including form, surface, lines and colours. Applications are reviewed by the Patent Office on the basis of relative novelty. The owner of a protected industrial design has the exclusive right of industrial exploitation. Protection lasts for five years and is renewable for an additional five-year period.

## *Utility models*

Utility models are also protected in Poland under the general patent law. Protection is available for '[a]ny new and useful solution of a technical nature affecting the shape, construction or permanent assembly of an object'. The procedures for obtaining utility model protection are similar to the procedures for provisional patent protection.

Utility model protection takes the form of a 'certificate of protection' and inventor's certificate. The owner of the certificate has the exclusive right to exploit the utility model throughout Poland.

## *Semiconductors*

Semiconductors are not currently protected under Polish law. However, consistent with its commitments to the US and to the EU, Poland is considering legislation to protect semiconductors.

# 25

# Project Finance
## *RZB-Austria*

While commercial bank finance can be made available for a maximum of three to five years for exports of capital goods, the banking market has difficulty in financing the longer terms required for project finance.

To circumvent this, it is generally necessary to work in partnership with multinational agencies such as the EBRD, IFC, MIGA or OPIC.

For British companies, the EBRD, with its headquarters in London, is the natural starting place in the quest for longer term project finance. The EBRD began operating in 1991 and has 55 member countries as shareholders. As with the World Bank and the IFC, it is a condition of membership that member countries will ensure there is sufficient availability of foreign exchange to serve any advances made by the EBRD. The political and transfer risk of such advances are, therefore, deemed to be largely mitigated, so that the Bank of England does not require commercial banks participating in such facilities to make provisions against their exposure and for this reason finance for periods up to ten years can be made available. Unlike the World Bank and the IFC in Washington, which deal with public sector infrastructure projects and commercial projects respectively, the EBRD is unique in being a multinational agency enjoying both franchises.

It is interesting to note that under the terms of its charter the EBRD can only provide up to one-third of the financial requirement for individual transactions, and that its minimum participation is ECU 5 million. Therefore, the minimum deal that can be structured directly with the EBRD is ECU 15 million. However, for transactions below this level the EBRD has negotiated agency lines with a number of banks.

In order to qualify, transactions should fall within the following parameters.

## BORROWERS

- Companies which have their head office in Poland and, in exceptional cases, holding companies which conduct their main business activities there.

- At least 51 per cent of a company's shares must be in private ownership or must be in the process of being privatised. (However, privatisations themselves are not being financed, ie EBRD funds are only available for the private sector industry rather than the public sector.)
- Local ownership is desirable (but not a pre-condition).

## LENDERS/AGENTS

- The EBRD is the 'lender of record' (to the outside world it appears as the lender).
- Banks with agency lines typically participate in loans up to 50–75 per cent of the amount advance and manage the loan approval process and negotiations with the borrower.

## PROJECT CHARACTERISTICS/SUITABILITY CRITERIA

In principle, special projects or investment programmes for the setting-up, modernisation or expansion of local companies will be financed by meeting the following criteria:

- 'classic' project finance (loan servicing out of project generated cash flow);
- independent assessment of the economic viability of the project;
- company contributes capital amounting to a minimum of 25–30 per cent of the project costs;
- no environmental risk;
- contributes to the economic development of the country in question (jobs etc).

## LOAN AMOUNT/COSTS

- Loan amount: maximum ECU 8 million (or any other freely convertible currency).
- Variable interbank rate of interest plus margin based on the general project risk and market conditions (the EBRD is not authorised to grant 'subsidised loans').
- Usual loan fees (up-front fee, agency fee, commitment fee).

## SECURITY

Usual security which can also be agreed with the EBRD on an individual basis (first mortgages, lien over machinery, charge over company shares, assignment of receivables, performance bonds etc).

## TERM

- The maximum term is ten years; the repayment period, however, is based on the predicted cash flow; short-term projects (five to seven years) have a better chance of succeeding.
- Yearly or half-yearly repayments.
- Period of grace: maximum two years.

## ADVANTAGES FOR THE BORROWER OR LENDER

- Reduction/elimination of transfer risk.
- Lower financing costs when compared to local currency financing.
- Cash flow need not be generated exclusively in hard currency.
- Approval process and negotiations with the borrower are considerably shorter than direct loan applications to the EBRD.

For larger deals, many of the above criteria will apply. Typically, the deal will be structured as an 'A' loan which the EBRD will keep for its own books (or sub-participate) and a 'B' loan which will be syndicated. The 'B' loan benefits from the same guaranteed availability of foreign exchange as the 'A' loan.

At the time of writing, the largest deal of this nature to be structured by the EBRD for Poland was Fiat Auto Poland's DM288 5 million facility for the expansion and modernisation of its car factory in Bielsko Biala. Fiat took the company over in 1992 and two years later sales had reached DM1.67 billion including exports of 150,000 Cinquecento cars to Western Europe. The EBRD subscribed a mix of equity (DM66 million) and senior debt (DM140 million) – with a 'B' tranche of the latter syndicated among a group of West European Banks. Additionally, a further DM66 million loan was arranged by the state-owned Polish Development Bank in which the European Investment Bank appeared as a participant.

Apart from the multinational agencies referred to above, a recent additional source of equity for investment in Poland is the Polish-American Enterprise Fund which maintains offices in New York and Warsaw. This was established in 1990 on the initiative of the US president and Congress. The fund, together with the Polish Private Equity Fund which it created as a source of parallel funding, has established a combined capital base of over US$340 million for equity investment. To date it has been responsible for disbursements in Poland totalling US$160 million, comprising 45 major investments and over 2700 small business loans.

# Investment Strategy
## BMF International Ltd

This chapter is aimed at providing potential investors with a practical guide and tips on investing in Poland. These are based on the real experience of having worked in Poland on both sides of the negotiating table – either representing a foreign investor or the Polish state treasury.

First one has to realise that although Poland is in the heart of Europe, it has been shielded for 50 years from developments that have occurred in the rest of Europe. As a result Poland is only just now beginning to learn how to administer a free market economy. At times, therefore, it can be difficult to equate the current mixture of a Western style professionalism with commercial naïvety and a sometimes irrational defence of local interests. History and people's experiences have influenced their way of thinking, resulting in the following:

- an appreciation for foreign goods;
- the fear that Western capital will buy all the best assets;
- an affinity for Western lifestyle and culture;
- taking responsibility for making decisions is risky;
- how do I personally benefit from my position?

To any new investor, Poland is full of potential difficulties. Typical problems include the following.

- **Unnecessary bureaucracy:** there are many institutions and groups involved in any transaction, and it is essential to target those who are the key decision makers. Potentially, all the following could be involved in a transaction:

    | | |
    |---|---|
    | Ministry of Privatisation | To get a general agreement |
    | Ministry of Industry or Agriculture | As the owner and policy maker |

| | |
|---|---|
| Ministry of Finance | Application for tax holidays etc |
| National Bank of Poland | Permission to hold foreign currency accounts |
| Ministry of Foreign Economic Relationships | Quotas on imports, permits |
| Management of company | To get a good insider's view of the target company |
| Workers' council | Represents workers in state-owned enterprise (SOE) |
| Local administration | Often acting as owner. Usually owner of land etc |

- **Political interference:** some members of political parties make an issue out of specific transactions.

- **High turnover of people in ministries:** often, within six months, whole teams of people can be rotated or rejected from a particular ministry, although sometimes the advisers do remain the same.

- **Achieving fair valuation:** this, on occasions, can create a problem. Using the asset replacement method, assets can be valued at many times more than their market worth. Companies can be quoted as having a value of P/Es as high as 20–30 while the potential investor is prepared to only pay a P/E of 3– 5.

- **Misinformation:** generally both investors and the Polish authorities do not pay enough attention to the problem of effective communication. Hence, a misconception of what a potential investor intends to do with the company may cause protests and difficulties with the relevant trade unions.

- **Rigidity of certain rules and regulations:** investors may well find that at first glance certain rules, for instance those governing environmental warranties, are highly unsatisfactory. During final negotiations, however, an acceptable solution to all parties can often be reached simply by rewording or clarifying certain issues.

- **Lack of good financial data:** under the Communist system there was no need for the production of what would be considered in the West as good financial data. An independent financial review is recommended early in the investment process.

- **Lack of clear objectives:** contradictory signals can sometimes be given as to what the Polish side wants to achieve through the completion of a certain transaction. This can be any one, or combination of, the following: maximise income to the state treasury, either on a short or long-term basis; raise new financing for the company; strengthen the management team; provide access to new export markets; provide Western technical and managerial know-how; retain maximum employment in a region suffering from high unemployment or under-development; carry out the privatisation at minimum cost.

- **Frequent changes to tax regulations:** this can be a troublesome area as sometimes the ground rules can shift even during the course of negotiations.
- **Poor confidentiality of negotiations:** quite often the progress or details of a transaction can appear in the media. Usually there is no malintention intended, it is just the result of an open attitude to the press.

None of these problems are insurmountable, however, and in fact they can create a certain barrier to entry that often allows those investors who persevere and finalise the transaction to reap extra benefits.

In order to succeed in making an investment in Poland, investors should consider the following points.

- **Constant local presence:** invariably there will be a need to keep on top of the situation – often on a daily basis. Use local advice – rediscovering the wheel is far more costly. The key is utilising personal contacts and establishing trust between the seller and buyer.
- **Flexibility:** no doubt a flexible approach needs to be taken as the final structure of the transaction may only arise after the generation of several alternative solutions.
- **Perseverance:** patience during the process will be essential – completion of a transaction can take anything up to between one to three years.
- **Properly managed information campaign:** this can be effected through meetings, written communications, use of mass media.
- **Perform your own analysis of the company:** as stated previously, it is strongly recommended that an investor should carry out their own due diligence.
- **Be prepared to repeat the message many, many times.**
- **Show full commitment at all times:** anything less will be seen as a lack of interest and will be treated accordingly.
- **Talk to all parties involved:** negotiate only with the decision makers.

- **Flexibility on employment guarantees:** build the social benefits and guarantees into the price.

In making an investment and deciding on the nature of a deal, it should be remembered that the same objectives – and structure – can be achieved through a variety of routes. For example, forming a joint venture with company A can be achieved through:

- 'liquidation' of company A and its contribution to a joint venture, with the foreign partner putting in cash;
- transfer of key assets (and liabilities) from company A to a joint venture company;
- transformation of company A into a joint stock company and issuing new shares taken up by the foreign investor.

In choosing the structure of the transaction the following comments apply.

- The formation of joint stock companies and/or liquidation of a company are governed by complex rules. For instance, the need to give shares to the employees, assume all liabilities (known and undisclosed), the need to advertise and hold a tender.
- The transfer of key assets (and certain liabilities) is an easier process. No tender is required and few permits. The Polish owner of the joint venture shares is a company not an authority representative. In addition, this process can limit the risk of undisclosed liabilities and the joint venture partner can choose the assets, as well as taking only the employees required. This is often, therefore, the best option for an investor but the state treasury does not favour this process since it leaves the Polish partner with the unrequired employees and assets which then need to be reorganised.

If the foreign investor starts discussions with a company at an early stage there is a chance of influencing the choice of the authority (owner) initiating the transaction. The authorities which undertake these transactions are:

- Ministry of Industry and Trade (MoIT), if it is a state-owned enterprise (SOE);
- Ministry of Privatisation (MoP) if the SOE is transformed into a joint-stock company;
- Voivoda's office (the voivoda can be regarded as the government's local representative). Ownership can be transferred from the MoIT to the voivoda;
- town/local authority (*gmina*). The process of communalisation may be enforced in the case when the target company is producing mostly for the local area;

- banks/ex-creditors, if the target company is heavily in debt, a so-called banking conciliatory procedure with a debt-to-equity swap can be introduced. The foreign investor can buy shares from ex-creditors or just debt and swap it into equity.

Choosing the right strategy regarding the owner is key since each of the above institutions will have their own objectives, agendas and methods.

Thus, for example, the MoIT will give a lot of priority to transactions important for the development of certain strategic sectors such as energy, pharmaceuticals, automotive, oil, steel etc. The MoIT, therefore, will be the best partner for a foreign investor wanting to make a deal in these kinds of sectors.

The MoP will give priority to large transactions generating income for the state treasury. It has the most skilled specialists but it also has major bottlenecks, and given the lengthy and formal procedures necessary to undertake a transaction with this ministry, fewer deals are completed.

The voivodas and town presidents tend to use a 'faster track' as the interest of the local community is at stake, especially in regard to the question of employment. However, there is the risk of the low experience of people with whom one will deal in these situations and this can have the effect of slowing the process down quite dramatically.

Creditors/banks are a very good partner. They have usually written off the debt, so are prepared to sell 'debt-for-equity' inexpensively and no government permits are required. This is a purely private deal and so can be completed very quickly. However, there is one drawback which that there may be a need to negotiate with a large number of shareholders.

It is worth repeating that a great deal of perseverance and flexibility will be required during negotiations and that working with a local partner is usually of great assistance.

# 27

# Investment Finance

## RZB-Austria

The financing of investments in Poland can be done in three ways: through the issuance of stock; borrowing from banks; or borrowing from the public by issuing bonds.

## FINANCING THROUGH ISSUANCE OF STOCK

The legal basis for public trading in securities is contained in the Law on Public Trading in Securities and Trust Funds of 22 March 1991 (Securities Act) with later amendments.

The shares are traded according to a single price system, where their value can fluctuate by a maximum of 10 per cent. Due to the recent developments on the stock exchange, where the inexperienced investors were driving the market down by selling their shares 'at market rate', an increasing number of brokerage houses want an amendment to be made forcing the investor to quote a sell or purchase price and disallowing the sell or purchase 'at market'. It is then possible that the 10 per cent brackets may be removed. Since the end of February it is possible to trade in warrants.

Any issuer wishing to introduce securities to public trading must obtain the consent of the Securities Commission to whom specific information on legal and financial issues must be provided.

The most important legal requirements, as specified by the Exchange Council, are as follows:

- the securities must be freely transferable;
- the value of shares must be at least Zl10 billion;
- at least 20 per cent of shares of the issuer must be subject to a public offer;
- relevant disclosure enabling an investor to assess the situation of the issuer and the rights arising out of the securities should be made.

Apart from the above requirements the issuer is obliged to publish quarterly, half yearly and yearly reports, as well as disclose all relevant information which may influence the investors' opinion. The failure to do so may cause the suspension of trading in the stocks of that issuer for up to three months or in the extreme the Stock Exchange Council may discontinue trading permanently.

The Securities Law and the Stock Exchange Rules do not impose any special restrictions on non-Polish entities.

In the last quarter of 1993 and the first quarter of 1994 this form of financing has been the most beneficial for the listed companies, due to the high cost associated with borrowings and the relatively low costs associated with acquiring capital on the Stock Exchange.

## FINANCING BY BANK LOANS

Due to the still high inflation in Poland, instability of the legal framework and undeveloped banking sector, this form of financing is very costly and difficult to acquire.

Banks are reluctant to finance investments through long-term due to the uncertainty regarding interest rate fluctuation and the fact that the Polish market is unpredictable. If a bank decides to finance an investment through debt the interest rates involved are very high, ranging from 5 to 7 per cent over one month Warsaw Inter Bank Offering Rate (WIBOR), which at present is around 30 per cent.

Big multinational companies can expect the banks to lower their interest rates if the companies will also channel all their business through them. If that happens the banks might offer a loan for as low as 1.5 to 2 per cent over one month WIBOR.

Foreign Exchange licensed banks may also grant hard currency loans.

## FINANCING THROUGH PUBLIC DEBT

The issuance of commercial bonds and bills is governed by the Bond Law of 27 September 1988. According to the law the amount of debt issued through bonds plus interest payable cannot exceed 50 per cent of equity or own unburdened funds. Guaranteed issues may exceed the above-mentioned limits.

Bonds can be issued on public subscription basis or through an offer to individual investors.

The issuer prior to the bond issue must publish a prospectus informing about purpose, amount, interest of bond, as well as the economic situation of the borrower. The financial statements, as is the case with all securities, have to be audited by a certified public auditor. The issuer has to publish his financial reports until full repayment of the debt.

Bond Law foresees debentures as registered securities or made out to bearer.

The bond market in Poland is very undeveloped. Such a situation is caused by a law which dates back to Communist rule. The tax structure of such financing is such that it stalled the formation of a secondary market of commercial debt on the stock exchange. Until the law is changed only small development of the market is foreseen.

## TAX INCENTIVES ASSOCIATED WITH INVESTMENTS

A new Decree of the Council of Ministers concerning new investment allowances was published on 25 January 1994 and covers investment expenditures incurred since 1 January 1994.

It is important to note that these allowances are in practice a form of accelerated depreciation and do not increase the amount ultimately deductible.

Companies will have the right to make deductions of investment outlays from profits before taxation only if:

1. in the previous year, a taxpayer has achieved profit of at least
   — 4 per cent of income, for companies in the agricultural, food processing or construction industries,
   — 8 per cent of income, for companies in all other fields of activity;
2. the taxpayer has no outstanding liabilities towards the state budget (ie taxes, social security contributions, contributions to the labour fund);
3. the expenditures have been documented by invoice by a VAT payer, or by customs duty documents, if the expenditure has been incurred on
   — purchase of licences, patents and transfer of know-how,
   — purchase of certain machinery and equipment,
   — payment of value of fixed assets on lease, if they are classified on the lessee's property.

For taxpayers involved in export – up to 50 per cent of income can be deducted, if one of the following conditions is met:

- that part of the income which is obtained from export exceeds 50 per cent of all income;
- the value of export services exceeds the equivalent of ECU 10 million.

For all other taxpayers, 25 per cent of the income may be deducted.

For tax purposes, only the higher of the normal depreciation and the investment allowance is deductible in any given tax year, and in no case can the aggregate of the investment allowance and subsequent depreciation exceed the initial value of investment.

The above-mentioned deductions of investment outlays does not apply to taxpayers already enjoying tax relief on the basis of other regulations, but will have the right as soon as their current tax relief expires.

# Setting up a Company
## Nabarro Nathanson

### INTRODUCTION

Under the Foreign Investment Law discussed in Chapter 11, foreign parties may only conduct business in Poland in the form of either a limited liability company or a joint stock company. The procedure of formation is more complex and time-consuming than in Anglo-Saxon jurisdictions and involves both a notary and a judge examining the company agreement (*umowa spółki* – in the case of a limited liability company) or statute (*statut* – in the case of a joint stock company) to ensure that the provisions of these documents conform with Polish law.

Polish company law dates from 1934 and not has been substantially revised since that time. The provisions in question were contained in the Commercial Code of that date and although the Code itself was repealed the provisions on companies remain in force to this day.

### LIMITED LIABILITY COMPANY

#### General

A Polish limited company (*Spółka z orgraniczoną odpowiedzialnością*) is modelled on a German *Gesellschaft mit beschränkter Haftung* (GmbH). It acquires legal personality upon registration in the commercial register held by a local court. As a general rule, the liability of its members is limited to the amount of their respective capital contributions. However, pursuant to recent legislation, shareholders of limited liability companies are proportionally liable for the unpaid tax obligations of the company.

The minimum share capital is Zl40 million which must be fully paid up on incorporation. The minimum value of each share is Zl1,500,000.

The main differences between a limited liability company and a joint stock company include (a) the amount of share capital, (b) the fact that a limited liability company cannot offer its shares to the public and (c) the fact that only a joint stock company may carry out certain activities such as banking or insurance.

### Incorporation procedure

It is possible for a limited liability company to have only one shareholder. However such a company cannot be a sole shareholder in another limited liability company.

The incorporation procedure will involve the following:

- the company agreement is prepared and executed as a notarial deed;
- the whole share capital is paid up;
- the governing bodies (the management board and supervisory board, if any) of the company are to be established; and
- the company is registered in the commercial register of the court in the location where the seat of the company is based. It is this final act of registration which creates the legal existence of the company. The application for registration must include any approval necessary under the Foreign Investment Law from the Ministry of Privatisation, powers of attorney from those who signed the notarial deed and specimen signatures of the members of the management board.

## JOINT STOCK COMPANY

### General

A Polish joint stock company (*Spółka Akcyjna*) is comparable to a German *Aktiengesellschaft* (AG). A joint stock company is the only business entity in Poland which is permitted to raise capital by means of a public flotation; such a flotation is regulated by the Securities Law of 1981, as amended.

### Incorporation procedure

The minimum share capital of Zl1 billion is required and the minimum nominal value of a share is Zl10,000.

There must be at least three founding shareholders unless the company is founded by national or local government, and the share capital must be divided into shares of an equal nominal value. Shares must be denominated in units of Zl10,000 or more.

While 'in-kind' contributions to capital must be fully paid up, only one-quarter of cash contributions need to be paid up prior to registration.

If any of the following are expected to apply:

- the issue of shares for contributions in kind,

- the acquisition in advance of registration of property rights (eg intellectual property, real estate), or
- the making of payments for services rendered in relation to the incorporation,

then the founders are obliged to prepare a written report detailing these matters.

This report must justify the transactions and the amount of remuneration involved, and identify the other parties involved. The report must be supported by an opinion from auditors as to whether all the relevant payments were justified. The auditors for this purpose will be appointed by the local registration court from a list kept for the purpose.

The report should be supported by original documents, invoices etc, and the auditors have the right to call for such further information as they require. The founders must respond to such requests, which must themselves be in writing, with written answers and explanations or further documents.

The auditors must provide two copies of their opinion to the registration court which will in turn provide a certified copy to the founders.

The statute of the company must be in the form of a notarial deed and be signed by the founding shareholders. The notarised deed must:

- identify the shareholders and specify the number and type of shares allocated to each of them;
- specify the issue price and deadline for payment;
- confirm the election of the first governing bodies; and
- if there is a founders' report and auditors' opinion, then the notarised deed(s) must state that each of the prospective shareholders signing the deed(s) is familiar both with the opinion and the contents of the report.

In addition, if capital is to be raised by public subscription, the statute must be published in a national newspaper.

The application for registration must be accompanied by:

- the notarised deed forming the company;
- a declaration signed by all members of the management board that all payments for shares have been made in accordance with the statute and that any contributions in kind are assured, and in the case of foreign investors that the contribution complies with the Foreign Investment Law;
- a statement as to the establishment and membership of the governing bodies;

- evidence that any necessary consents have been obtained;
- specimen signatures of the members of the management board, either signed before the court, or authenticated by a notary.

If the capital was raised by public subscription, the following documents must also accompany the application:

- the prospectus;
- the minutes of the 'organisational meeting' (special shareholders; meeting held following a public subscription);
- a list of subscribers, showing the shares allocated to each and the amounts of any payments received;
- bank statements evidencing the payments;
- the founders' report and the auditors' opinion (where appropriate);
- the report of the committee elected at the 'organisational meeting'.

An important point to note is that anyone who acts on behalf of the company prior to its incorporation is personally liable for their actions. Such liability, if there is more than one such person, is joint and several.

In the event of irregularities being discovered after registration, the registration court can (either on its own initiative or at the instigation of an interested party) give notice to the company requiring it to correct these irregularities by a deadline set by the court. Failure to comply will lead to a fine or, if the defects are 'materially significant for the continued existence of the company', dissolution. A company of five years' standing cannot, however, be dissolved on the grounds of pre-registration irregularities.

*Part IV*

# Case Studies

*Case Study 1*

# Elektrim

Following the profound macro-changes that have occurred within the economy since 1989 many Polish companies have had to entirely reorient their activities and strategy in order to operate in the new business environment that has been evolving. A good example of a large Polish company which has had to reorganise its business focus radically in order to compete in this newly competitive market place is Elektrim.

The following case study demonstrates how the management in Elektrim have successfully restructured their company so as to be able to face the challenges that lay before them and benefit from the opportunities that are now presenting themselves.

## BACKGROUND

Elektrim was founded in 1945 as one of several foreign trade organisations (FTOs), which were established as the sole entities responsible for the import and export of goods and services for a specific industrial sector in Poland. Elektrim's initial business was focused on the import of electrotechnical equipment needed for the rebuilding of Poland's post-war power generation capacity, but over time the enterprise began to export Polish products in this sector to both Comecon and non-Comecon countries. In 1986 the government decided to break the monopoly of the FTOs which meant that their customers were no longer required to do business through the FTOs. Therefore if the FTOs were to survive it required them to diversify into other business areas.

## THE EARLY 1990S

Elektrim had traditionally acted as an agent for either the supplier or the purchaser in the power sector in Poland. Prior to market liberalisation, the main source of income for Elektrim was commission received on brokering deals between its international contacts and local companies. With markets opening up, traditional client companies had the opportunity to make direct contact with the end purchaser and to handle sales of their products themselves. Simultaneously international competition started to take interest in the central European markets and its low cost manufacturing base, and began to make acquisitions in Poland. This posed a huge challenge to Elektrim – respond quickly or slowly get squeezed out of the market.

## ELEKTRIM'S RESPONSE

Elektrim confronted this issue by taking the bold strategic decision to keep its client base by aggressively vertically integrating upstream its core business areas, and moving into manufacturing and distribution. It defined its core areas as:

- power equipment;
- electrical machinery apparatus;
- telecommunications;
- cables;
- lighting equipment.

Elektrim's target acquisitions were companies with which it already had long-standing relationships. In this way Elektrim was able to act fast, cutting further due diligence and acquisition time. Through its strong cash flow and its ability to raise additional finances, Elektrim has been able to implement these transactions very quickly and by the end of 1993 the company had acquired shareholdings in 87 domestic companies.

Management recognised the risks in such an aggressive policy by pointing out that Elektrim's transformation had to be radical as there was a greater risk associated with complacency. One example of Elektrim's financial acumen was the 80 per cent acquisition in 1991 of Mostostal Warszawa, a specialist steel construction company, from the Ministry of Privatisation. Two years after their purchase Elektrim floated 32 per cent of Mostostal Warszawa on the WSE and made substantial profits, in dollar terms.

The company's strategy to date has focused on acquisitions in their core business sectors. For instance, in its cables business, Elektrim has become a major European player by beating major international competition in buying Poland's key cable manufacturer, Bydgoskie Fabryki Kabli, and is looking to strengthen this position through the acquisition of other significant cable manufacturers in Poland. In the electrical machinery sector, Elektrim has already bought one of the principal electric motor manufacturers and is currently bidding for another.

A key feature of the acquisitions in the core businesses has been the additional financial resources Elektrim has committed to invest heavily and restructure these companies. This strategy has ensured that Elektrim has maintained a stable and healthy client base, while simultaneously giving its acquisitions a secure distribution channel, and access to finance for future investments and growth.

In a move intended to create synergies with existing business areas, Elektrim has also purchased one of the leading Polish lime producers whose product is key in the desulphurisation of emissions from power plants. Moving into the environmental protection and emission control business is a logical step for Elektrim, especially given its presence in the power sector, and the urgent requirement for Poland to make huge investments in this area, in order to bring its power stations in line with Western standards.

ABB has taken a 10 per cent stake of Elektrim, and with ABB's manufacturing capability in Poland and Elektrim's distribution capacity there will be many opportunities in the future for the two companies to work together. Elektrim is also looking to consolidate its relationship with Telekommunikacja Polska, for which it acts as principal supplier, through a series of joint ventures, thus bolstering further the company's presence in a rapidly expanding market.

## THE FUTURE

In the short and medium term Elektrim's strategy is to focus on the following areas.

- to consolidate, integrate and strengthen existing domestic core manufacturing businesses;
- to diversify into new growth areas of the Polish economy;
- to develop the capability to take part in large infrastructure projects. To this end Elektrim has joined with Bank Przemyslowo-Handlowy, Stalexport and Exbud to form the Polish Economic Consortium. The intention is that together they will be able to provide domestic financial power to compete against foreign bidders. One such project which the consortium is targeting are the planned 2500 km of motorways which are planned to be built in Poland.

Another innovative area which Elektrim has worked on is an incentive bonus scheme for employees. This is an entirely new concept for Polish employees who never before had to take responsibility for their output. Under this incentive scheme employees are rewarded for increased profitability which has ensured that all departments within Elektrim are united in trying to grow the company.

## PRIVATISATION

In September 1990 Elektrim was transformed into a joint stock company as a precursor to privatisation and its shares floated on the WSE in March 1992 at a price of Zl70,000. By the end of July 1994 its share price stood at Zl1,160,000 (post a 2:1 split), giving the company a market cap of US$310 million. At the end of 1993 Elektrim had an asset base (adjusted) of US$290 million. During the year Elektrim had sales of US$350 million and pre-tax profits of US$62 million. The company has a staff of 650. Elektrim now ranks as one of the leading private companies in Poland, it is the most actively traded company on the WSE and is widely considered to be one of Poland's blue chips.

## Case Study 2

# Pilkington

George Murray, recently retired as Vice President, Eastern Europe and Keith Beckett, Technical Director Europe for Pilkington plc, led a joint venture team to Poland for over three and a half years and the resulting company is now building Poland's first float glass plant in Sandomierz, the site of an existing sheet glass manufacturer.

The joint venture, established in September 1993 between Pilkington and the Government of Poland, leaves Pilkington 40 per cent of the equity, with 30 per cent belonging to the Polish Government for contributing the plant and 30 per cent initially shared by financial institutions; the International Finance Corporation and the EBRD. The EBRD's share, as bridge equity, was then passed to the New Europe East Investment Fund, as planned between all those concerned. There is a 60:40 debt:equity ratio.

Pilkington Sandoglass Sp zo.o is the company that will operate the new plant, headed by Jonas Borup, who was previously chief executive of Lahti, Pilkington's float glass company in Finland, and will produce 140,000 tonnes of glass per annum. The sheet plant has a capacity of 106,000 tonnes. It is one of the largest Polish privatisations and was the largest single investment in Poland by the IFC and the largest private sector investment by the EBRD.

The decision to enter the market was influenced by the fact that Poland has a population of 40 million and a well established glass making industry but no modern plant. The project, amounting to £100m, brings modern float technology to replace sheet, which is a process used hardly at all outside the Third World and whose products are now considered inadequate for any applications, such as the automotive industry and for modern architecture. Pilkington calculated that if no float plant was built by 1995, Poland would be importing at least £30m worth of glass each year. In fuel consumption terms, float is approximately twice as efficient as sheet so there are hard currency savings for Poland on every square metre of glass produced.

The project is for a 'genuine' joint venture, ie it is not purely a foreign investment with a token Polish presence. There are currently 650 people on site constructing the float plant, which will be finished in September 1995.

The two existing sheet plants on the site will close, one before and one after the float plant comes into operation. The float plant will retain part of the sheet plant, where the raw materials are processed, upgrading it to fit float glass requirements. Equipment for the plant will be imported from the UK, Europe and the USA. Thirty million pounds of goods and services will be supplied from the UK alone.

All local work is let on contract to Polish suppliers and construction companies, eg civil engineering, roads, steelwork, painting, mechanical and electrical erection. Pilkington have undertaken to improve the local infrastructure as part of the project, including improving the roads around the plant, and putting £250,000 into improving the water supply to the plant and the local community.

When negotiations for the project began, Pilkington was directed to the Foreign Investment Agency, who insisted that power had been decentralised and they should be dealing directly with the sheet plant at Sandomierz. Under the communist system, the plant belonged to the Government and sure enough, after a while, they had to return to Warsaw. Their official contact in the Government was the Minister of Industry, but they were also dealing with the Ministry of Privatisation and the Treasury, the County (Vojevoid) Government and the town council.

The Vojevoid was particularly keen to ensure the plant would conform to the strict environmental regulations for this historic region. Pilkington therefore prepared thoroughly, by making sure that the banks (particularly the EBRD) and their experts from around the world fully exchanged views.

Labour also became a difficult issue; in a genuine joint venture the labour is in place and cannot be trained in advance as with a greenfield site. The existing labour force brought both the advantage of industry knowledge and the disadvantage of experience in outdated processes with a different industrial culture and assumptions about the way industry should be, based on years of state monopoly. Sales, marketing and distribution systems had to be transformed and a new way of thinking invested in the labour forces. This is time consuming and makes great demands on the human resources of the Western partner.

As sheet is a relatively labour-intensive process, float glass will necessarily bring labour reductions in the plant at Sandomierz where 1200 people currently work. Jobs will be created downstream of the manufacturing plant however, in the manufacture of added value products and in wholesaling and distribution. The project contains £1m to create new jobs in the Sandomierz area.

Pilkington decided on a totally open approach in negotiations with the Government and the Workers' Council. They had to defend their beliefs and values, they declared and defended their sales forecasts, shared their view of how the industry would develop in the next decade and talked about the demise of sheet glass (challenging the plant management view head-on). They discussed the lack of finance available to upgrade the sheet glass business, domestic and foreign competition and the necessary improvements in quality. Generally during discussions the Eastern side sits down to negotiate in technology, but Westerners want to talk about funding and developing markets in which technology may or may not be a fundamental part of a sensible deal.

Financial, legal, environmental and technical experts were continually flying to and from Poland, pushing to meet deadlines and solve problems and misunderstandings which invariably occurred during such complex negotiations. The hard preparatory work and the experts' commitment, with the support from the EBRD and the IFC, eventually ensured that agreements were reached.

Demand for glass in Poland is twice as much as the float glass plant could supply. Currently, demand is met by the sheet plants and 15 per cent is met by imports. Pilkington imports glass from their plant in Sweden. From the float glass plant the finished glass will be despatched by road, using local lorry companies, to the rest of the country where Pilkington will have distribution warehouses in strategic areas. All the glass produced is expected to go to the domestic Polish market for use particularly in double-glazing, automotive products and white goods. Eventually, all Polish sheet glass plants will close as a result of the introduction of float glass.

## Case Study 3

# Cadbury Schweppes

The worldwide confectionery market accounts for £145 billion. There is a large number of people with a sweet tooth in Central and Eastern Europe, representing one-fifth of the total market.

To Cadbury Schweppes, who had a £416 million profit last year, Central and Eastern Europe looked promising. In 1992 they looked at the whole region and split it into three sections; the East, including the CIS, where at that time the economies were quite underdeveloped; the South, which included areas at war or with poor economies; and Central Europe, which was moving ahead very positively.

Within Central Europe, a particularly promising market is Poland, with its large population of 38 million and economic growth which was already evident in 1992. A large proportion of the economy is private and there is a large confectionery market, with a volume of 179,000 tonnes.

The next decision was whether to invest in an existing company or a 'greenfield' project. Looking at the pros and cons of each, it was decided that the highest technology could be used with the highest productivity in a 'greenfield' site, suitable for a long-term investment.

When looking for a suitable area within Poland, Cadbury's saw that the wealthier areas were in the south/west where the population was concentrated. In March 1993, they visited a site at Wroclaw, in an area designated for industrial development, near a main motorway interchange, useful for distribution.

Negotiations were mostly held on the local level. The development of the site is the responsibility of the local mayor and his committee, who were involved in 95 per cent of the negotiations. The only approach to Warsaw was to obtain permission to buy the land, now wholly owned by Cadbury Schweppes.

Other helpful organisations throughout the investment process were the British Embassy in Poland, the Polish Embassy in London and PAIZ, the State Foreign Investment Agency. Negotiations with the local people of the Kobierzyce commune were the most successful. Although they have a very different negotiating technique, they were very businesslike and are sticking to their side of the agreement. One reason for choosing the site at Wroclaw was the good impression the local people gave and that they got things done. It was also useful to have local consultants, who dealt with the local authorities. On the whole the process was quicker, kept at the local level.

Plans were made to build a one-storey factory, which has proved to be most efficient in other countries. Most existing confectionery factories in Central and Eastern Europe are four to ten storeys in the middle of cities with no room for expansion or distribution. Construction started in mid-September 1993 by a Polish company working for a British contractor and the factory will be run by a Polish team with one ex-pat.

The infrastructural side has been taken care of, the telephone authority has promised to install 15 lines to the factory and the mayor is responsible for the supply of water and electricity. Temporary supplies were available for the construction of the plant, which was delivered on time and proved the mayor's efficiency.

The investment should be complete by the end of 1994 and is part of the Cadbury Schweppes European strategy, which has already acquired businesses in Spain, France and Germany. The Polish project will continue a chain across Europe. When Poland joins the EU, it will mean an extension to the overall European market, with the Polish factory supplying some products to the rest of Western Europe. Quality standards will be maintained and have to be good if not better in the East, because Polish consumers are sensitive to low quality dumping from the West.

Cadbury Schweppes are the sole shareholders, avoiding the trouble of a minority holder who would be concerned to receive dividends. By being 100 per cent shareholders, Cadbury's can look to the long term and invest for several years without profit, which is bearable for the parent company but might not be acceptable for minority holders. This is the advantage over joint ventures, which are more restrictive.

There are many difficulties to be experienced in Poland, like trying to find someone who knows the jurisdiction and can tell you who you need to see to get things done. It is difficult sometimes to define the parameters within which you have to work. For example, there were no environmental specifications stating what would be allowed in effluent.

This lack of certainty means that it is difficult to plan effectively. Cadbury's needed to know when the investment would be complete, as the confectionery market shows seasonal fluctuations; people tend to eat more chocolate in the winter months around Christmas and less in the summer. It is therefore better to start up a factory before the autumn. Timing is critical and unfortunately few people in Poland have a sense of the importance of time.

One particularly difficult issue is corruption. With all the hurdles to face, and permissions and approvals to be obtained, it is very tempting for companies to pay to get things done. Cadbury's have resisted this temptation and have succeeded in making their investment.

The opportunities in Poland are many. It is politically stable, and although governments come and go, their policies are solid and they continue along the path of economic reform. Companies new to the market should look at local communities and avoid concentrating only on meetings with ministries. A lot of patience and persistence is needed.

Now is the time to enter the Polish market, as the 'window of opportunity' is closing. The costs are still reasonable but are rising, television advertisements are cheap and the people are responsive to them, which is important when establishing a brand name. A 'greenfield' investment is a good way into the market with 100 per cent ownership, a joint venture is fine if the partner actually brings something into it. It is difficult to find a suitable partner for consumer goods particularly, as existing confectionery factories had no sales and distribution network, they simply produced and waited for customers to drive up and take the product away. Existing companies are often overmanned and although joint ventures often have an agreement for two to three years guaranteed employment, the excess labour will be redundant in the end.

The Cadbury Schweppes investment is on track and despite the problems, it is the fastest 'greenfield' investment ever made by Cadbury Schweppes anywhere in the world.

*Case Study 4*

# Unicorn Poland

Information systems within Polish operations have been transformed out of all recognition in the past four years. Where, for instance, the country's financial linchpin, the National Bank of Poland, used to have a higgledy-piggledy collection of stand-alone computers, it now has a standardised network delivering consistent flows of information.

Poland is also being increasingly linked into international networks. Despite shortcomings in the communications infrastructure, there is no reason why operations should not follow the lead of ABB, the Swedish–Swiss engineering conglomerate, whose Zamech factory at Elblag is now directly connected to the group's marketing efforts worldwide by virtue of Lotus Notes.

Installing such systems has not been plain sailing. At the advent of economic reform in 1990, the market for computers was generally made up of clones from the Far East using pirated software. Polish users had lived in a culture in which copying software was not frowned on and there was no appreciation of intellectual property rights. Right at the beginning of the reform process, there was even an expectation that the West might simply pass on software free of charge.

In this free for all, there was no standardisation: a Polish version of DOS did not exist; characters on keyboards came in 17 different configurations; and none of the standard commands, such as save or file, had Polish equivalents. Added to uncertainties about getting paid, it was small wonder that the major international hardware and software suppliers were reluctant to make any commitment to the market.

Unicorn Poland Sp z o.o. has played a pioneering role in developing the Polish software market. It is an Anglo-Polish venture which has identified and packaged the software most appropriate to the developing needs of Polish corporates.

The company has become the leading translator of software into Polish, introducing local versions of programmes for Dos and Windows. It has even introduced the first Polish spell checker for a Western translated word processor – no mean feat in a language where the declension of nouns varies.

Unicorn is also one of the three principal software distributors with a network of 200 dealers across the country. By 1994 it had grown into a company with a £2 million turnover employing 43 staff in Warsaw and Poznan supported by a team of contractors.

It is run from London on a sophisticated computer link by the company's founder and managing director, Stanislaw Staruch, who left Poland for the UK in 1976. On the introduction of the Convertibility Law in 1990, he set up Unicorn with the original intention of distributing software packages for project management. He soon realised that the market was not ready for this.

A look at what was being pirated told him that Polish companies were looking for relatively simple business applications, such as spreadsheets and profit-and-loss accounts. The wrong way to meet this demand, Stanislaw Staruch felt, was to devise sophisticated marketing strategies from Germany. Instead, he formed a joint venture with what he describes as a typical Polish company of the late 1980s: ' a jack of all trades with talented employees but no funding'. It had the merit of having a software arm, contracted to Polish social security with the brief of writing accounting software for foreign pensions to cooperate with 200 banks.

The next step for Unicorn was to approach Lotus, who had no presence in the market at all to market their 1-2-3 spreadsheet. Agreement was reached by January 1991, although Lotus were unwilling to put up any finance.

The Lotus 1-2-3 was the first software package to be launched Western style in Poland. The demonstrations given at the leading information technology (IT) trade fair were so popular that the fire brigade were called in to marshal the crowds. The subsequent roadshow round Poland was a sell-out.

Priced at US$495, Lotus 1-2-3 was aimed at the corporate, not the personal market. The selling cycle proved to be a drawn-out process, resulting in orders perhaps 18 months later. Whereas in the West there is an understanding of the capabilities of a package, the learning curve was much longer in Poland. Uncertainty also brought out a bureaucratic mentality which demands that everything be signed in triplicate, so nobody bears individual responsibility for a decision. One of Unicorn's most successful marketing initiatives has been to run relatively inexpensive introductory courses on the benefits information systems offer companies.

The success of Lotus 1-2-3 encouraged Unicorn to introduce Lotus Notes, a network communications package which provides a multi-task environment for companies. Its launch generated less excitement, partly because the idea of a network extending further than the office next door is still fairly alien to Polish managers.

All the latest software is now available in Poland, supported by high quality magazines full of advertising. The market is no longer simply a matter of straightforward trading. Although it remains highly price sensitive, Stanislaw Staruch feels that scope for value-added services is developing.

Unicorn's management team is broadly the same as when the joint venture was set up. Programmers may not be paid the highest rate, but retention is high on account of plenty of opportunities for training and travel. Secretarial positions have proved the most difficult of all to fill: in the old days, the position was split between pools, copy machinists, coffee makers and telephone receptionists. Getting someone with the organisational nous to carry out the whole range of office duties is difficult.

In 1991, Unicorn insisted its dealers made a US$2500 minimum purchase as a signal of good intent. The market has moved on considerably since then with Microsoft distributors, for instance, regarding anyone who buys in stock as a dealer.

Unicorn has a sound base in which to build in Poland. Until recently it was the only Lotus Notes value added reseller in Eastern Europe, as well as acting as an intermediary for other major international suppliers of software such as Microsoft. As well as playing a key role in the packaging and presentation of software products, it is now also one of the largest translators of software into East European languages. Stanislaw Staruch foresees that this expertise will act as a platform for activity in not only Russia, but in selling skills in setting up communications networks back to Western Europe.

After gathering dust for two years, the Lotus Notes package really started to take off in Poland during 1994. Although it is still best to communicate during off-peak hours because of shortcomings in the telecommunications systems, ambitious operations in Poland are rapidly becoming plugged into the most sophisticated international networks.

# Appendices

*Appendix 1*

# Opportunities by Sector

## *BMF International Ltd*
Compiled with the help of the Ministry of Industry and Trade

### AGRICULTURE

Although Poland's topography, climate and soil are generally favourable for farming, there are significant regional variations. The more productive agricultural land is situated in the north-west and south-east of Poland, where state farms are dominant. The central region is also a highly productive agricultural area, with horticulture predominant. Polish agriculture accounted for 7.3 per cent of GDP (in 1992). The agricultural sector encompasses the production of fruit, vegetables, grains and livestock.

Polish farm land (18,741,000 ha) constitutes 60 per cent of the country, of which 75.9 per cent is owned by the private sector whilst 24.1 per cent is state-owned.

Polish individual farms are small in size – on average 7.1 ha, with 53 per cent of farms under 5 ha, 82 per cent of farms under 10 ha and only 6 per cent of farms 15 ha or larger. There are regional differences in the size of private farms, eg in the northern province of Olsztyn the average size is 12.4 ha, whereas in the south-eastern district of Bielskie, the average size is 2.6 ha. Conversely, state farms average 2171 ha while agricultural co-operatives average 342 ha.

Farmers and their families comprise 38 per cent of Poland's total population, but only about 20 per cent of the population generate their income exclusively from farming. The agricultural sector employs 27 per cent of the country's workforce.

Despite the relatively small farms, Poland is a significant producer of horticultural and grain goods, being ranked first among East and Central European countries in vegetable and fruit production and highly placed among Western European countries. In Europe, for example, Poland ranks first in the production of currants and strawberries, second in the production of rye, oats and potatoes, fourth in the production of apples, rape and oil-yielding rape, and fifth in the production of sugar beet and tobacco. Worldwide, Poland ranks second in production of rye, third in production of potatoes and fourth in production of oats (1992 statistics). These high yields are attributable more to the large amount of arable land allocated for production rather than to the yield rates of specific crops. (Poland also ranks third in pork production and fifth in milk production in Europe.)

Poland's agricultural sector is labour intensive in comparison to those of Western Europe. The level of mechanisation has been greatest in the state-owned farms, and domestic agricultural machinery and equipment manufacturers have been specifically geared to serve the requirements of this sector. Therefore, the strong demand from small private farms is currently only being met through imported machinery – leaving a market niche for a foreign investor who can produce locally using modern technology.

There is a significant number of tractors – on average in 1991 there was one tractor for 16 ha of arable land. The usage varies, depending on the ownership structure and location, for example, state-owned farms average 44 ha, agricultural co-operatives 32 ha and private farms 14 ha. In comparison the average usage of a tractor in Spain is for 40 ha, Bulgaria 120 ha, Netherlands 10.6 ha. It is a similar story for combine harvesters – one machine for 80 ha of grain, while the average combine harvester density in Austria is 26 ha, Spain 147 ha and Bulgaria 206 ha.

Fourteen companies in Poland specialise in tractor production – 11 are state-owned, of which ZPC Ursus is the largest manufacturer, and 3 smaller private firms. There is only one combine harvester manufacturer in Poland (Bizon), which is currently undergoing a restructuring programme. Agricultural research institutes are traditionally of a high standard.

One of the main problems in the past has been the lack of an effective financing system for farmers which would allow them to become more efficient by buying modern machinery and fertilisers. (The high interest rates were unsustainable for farmers in such a seasonal industry.) However, this issue was addressed in April 1994 by the introduction of new preferential credits for farmers as organised by the Agency of Restructuring and Modernisation of Agriculture.

## AUTOMOTIVE

The Polish vehicle manufacturing industry includes 120 companies, employing jointly 83,000 people and is responsible for 2.7 per cent of the output of the industrial sector. Of these firms 62 are state-owned and 58 are private.

The main car manufacturers are as follows.

- Fiat Auto Poland is the largest domestic manufacturer with plants in Bielsko and Tychy in southern Poland. It manufactured 195,000 Cinquecento cars and 66,000 Fiat 126s in 1993, and in 1994 started assembly of the Uno.

- FSO, located in Warsaw, manufactures the Polonez range of medium-sized passenger and utility vehicles, and recently signed a joint venture agreement with Opel to make the Astra sedan.
- FS Lublin assembles the Peugeot 405 from CKD kits and manufactures its own brand of light delivery vans.
- VW Transporter vans are assembled by Volkswagen Poznań.

The main commercial vehicle and bus manufacturers are Jeicz, Star and Autosan. All three are state-owned enterprises which have been through the restructuring process and are engaged in discussions with investors concerning their privatisation. (At the time of writing, Jelcz was about to be bought by the Zasada-Mercedes company). The government is adopting a number of measures aimed at enticing investment in the commercial vehicle sector. These include high import duties, a ban on the import of commercial vehicles more than three years old and preferences for domestic manufacturers in public sector procurement.

There are currently around 6,900,000 passenger cars registered in Poland, ie circa 200 per 1000 inhabitants. In 1993 265,300 new cars were sold on the Polish market of which 76,300 were imported and 189,000 domestic – mainly the Polonez, Fiat Cinquecento and Fiat 126. The popularity of domestic vehicles is mainly attributable to their price, not being encumbered with high border taxes and having attractive financing schemes.

The main importer was Fiat with over 22,000 vehicles followed by the VW Group, Open, Ford and Renault.

A duty-free import contingent of 31,750 vehicles manufactured in the EU, caused protests from Japanese, Korean and Czech manufacturers, and explains the lack of Japanese firms among the main importers.

In the next five years the market for passenger cars is expected to double as purchasing power increases and old East European vehicles are replaced by new cars.

There are 1,200,000 commercial vehicles registered in Poland, mostly of Polish and East European origin. The expected future trend is for a shift towards smaller and lighter vehicles, and a relative decrease in the number of heavy lorries.

## BREWING

Poland had 76 breweries in operation in 1993. The potential for significant growth in this industry is reflected by:

- the size of the domestic market in Poland – there are about 25 million people of working age;
- the market is relatively under-developed. The strong tradition of vodka drinking is reflected by the currently low annual per capita

consumption of beer in Poland (45:1) in comparison with its neighbours – Germans (144:1) and Czechs (132:1);

- the progress of privatisation in the industry. Out of 76 breweries, 10 major ones have already been privatised, some through listing on the Warsaw Stock Exchange (eg Żywiec, Okocim), some through trade sales (eg Elblag, Koszalin) and the rest through employee buy-outs (eg Warszawa, Lublin). In 1993 about 50 per cent of beer production came from private breweries;

- following the introduction of higher duties, the sharp fall in imports from 3 million hl in 1990–1 to 0.7–0.8 hl in 1993;

- the significant interest expressed by major international beer companies in entering the Polish brewing market. Some of them, such as Brewpole Pty, AMS Anlagen Planung, Heineken and Braun und Brunnen have already made some investments.

The larger breweries are concentrated in three regions: southern Poland (the Bielsko, Kraków, Tarnów voivodships), the Silesian area and western/south-western region (Poznań, Wrocklaw and Ople voivodships). This geographical spread originated from the nineteenth century.

The total production of beer in Poland has been fluctuating in the last few years between 13.3 million hl and 15 million hl.

The industry is quite fragmented with no truly national breweries. Unlike Western Europe the production volumes per brewery are relatively low – there are few breweries which produce over 1 million hl per annum – Elbrewery (1.53 million hl), Browary Wielkopolskie (1.22 million hl) and Browary Tyskie (1.08 million hl). Over the next few years the industry is likely to see an on-going process of market consolidation and the introduction of national distribution networks.

# CHEMICAL

The modern Polish chemical industry has a long history dating back to the beginning of the nineteenth century, when Ignacy Lukasiewicz drilled the world's first oil wells. Today the chemical industry represents circa 10 per cent of total industrial output.

During the last four years of economic transformation the chemical industry has suffered less than other sectors of industry. This can be explained by:

- relatively modern technologies;
- stable positions in the domestic and international markets;
- low labour cost of production;

- significant deposits of chemical raw materials (coal, sulphur, limestone, gypsum, salt);
- long-term relationships with internationally well-known companies, for instance, Shell, Hoechst, BASF, Ciba-Geigy, Norsk Hydro, Kemira Oy etc.

There are around 400 large chemical plants in Poland of which more than 50 per cent have been commercialised. Already three large companies manufacturing detergent and cleaning agents have been privatised through mergers with foreign strategic partners: Pollena Bydgoszcz (Unilever), Pollena Nowy Dwór Mazowiecki (Benkiser) and Pollena Racibórz (Henkel). The leading Polish paints and varnish manufacturer Polifarb Cieszyn was publicly floated on the WSE as the first company from this sector. Currently, three other joint stock companies are well advanced in the flotation process: Jelfa (pharmaceutical), FFiL Wroclaw (paints and varnishes) and Prochem (a design office for the chemical industry), while other companies such as the Dębica Tyre Company and the Pharmaceutical Factory Polfa-Kutno are also being prepared for public sale.

To date only a few Western companies have decided to set up 'greenfield' production facilities, one such example being Solco–Basel (pharmaceuticals) who is investing up to US$35 million.

The largest industrial complexes such as Plock Refinery and Petrochemical Plant, Gdańsk Refinery or Pulawy Fertiliser Manufacturer have already been commercialised, some of which will be privatised through the National Investment Funds as well as the more conventional privatisation routes.

During the last three years, despite the demanding financial conditions given by Polish banks, several new investment projects have been completed, including a new unit for urea prilling in Pulawy Fertiliser Manufacturer, and the revamping and extension of ammonia and synthetic gas production in Kędzierzyn Fertiliser Company (regarded as one of the most modern production units in the world).

It is evident that the Polish government is very keen to see continued development in certain sectors of this industry. These include: refinery and petrochemicals, pharmaceuticals, paints and varnishes, fine chemicals, tyres and rubber products – particularly for the motor-car industry.

## COAL

Poland has historically been one the leading hard coal producers in the world. In 1993, it had an output of around 130 million tonnes – of which 25 million tonnes were exported, making it the largest producer in Europe and the sixth largest in the world. At the end of 1993 it consisted of 73 deep mines – mostly concentrated in the Upper Silesian region – and employed a workforce of 305,000. Over 60 per cent of Poland's energy requirements are met through domestic hard coal and, taken together with its exports, gives some indication of the importance of the industry to the Polish economy now and for the foreseeable future.

The economic transformation of Poland induced a fall in demand in energy and through this a decrease in the requirement for hard coal. This, together with previous governments' policies of trying to help Polish industry get over the economic transformation by keeping energy prices low through the suppression of the price of coal, had a dramatic effect on the profitability of this sector.

To help the industry face this crisis and restructure itself, the industry was reorganised in the first half of 1993 into six coal companies and one holding company – all taking the form of joint stock companies owned by the state. (The most uncompetitive mines were put into liquidation.) In addition, domestic coal prices were brought up to parity with world levels. Since then these companies have been deeply engaged in radical financial and operational restructuring – including a wide-ranging debt write-off scheme, and the divestiture and privatisation of non-core assets. This strategy has already shown some benefits as positive operating profits were recorded, for the first time in months, at the end of 1993. It is expected, however, that this painful consolidation process will carry on for the foreseeable future as the industry continues to downsize to meet lower domestic energy demand and tries to become more internationally competitive.

## CONSTRUCTION

Construction is one of the most important sectors in the Polish economy. This sector declined considerably after the economic transformations in 1989. The main reasons for this significant decline lie in the discontinuation of subsidies by the state as well as the lack of affordable financing. The average annual number of apartments built during 1986–90 was 170,100. However, this declined to an annual average of 134,200 in 1991 and 127,100 in 1992. The main reason for this fall was that co-operatives and state-owned firms, traditionally the largest builders and investors, could not adapt to the new market conditions.

This sharp decline in the fortunes of the large state-owned companies is currently being filled by middle-sized private firms, which are very flexible in terms of meeting customers' requirements, the implementation of new technologies and new sources of finance. Through their intervention, previously unknown financial instruments such as mortgage loans have been introduced into the Polish economy. This change in the structure of the industry in 1990–2 is reflected in a 98 per cent increase in the number of privately owned companies and firms, and a 137 per cent increase in the number of joint venture companies.

Construction was responsible for 9.2 per cent of GDP in 1990 rising to 10.23 per cent in 1991. The number of employees in this sector declined from 1.24 million in 1990 to 1.14 in 1992 (which is 7.4 per cent of the total labour force). During this time there was also a large migration of employees from state-owned firms to private companies, which by the end of 1992 employed 70 per cent of the total workforce in this sector.

The market for construction materials and services has also seen structural change. This has primarily been led by many Poles still wanting either to own their own house or improve their current dwelling, but not being able to afford traditional construction techniques. Therefore, they are increasingly turning to 'new-tech' construction and many companies import American or Canadian building technologies. However, on average there are still more than three people per one apartment and the average living surface per person is 17.9 m$^2$. Only 10.7 per cent of buildings were built after 1979.

Nevertheless, the future for the construction industry in Poland looks bright. Apart from the pent-up demand for housing, a great deal of industrial construction is also planned. For instance, the Polish government has decided to start building a network of motorways, an investment calculated to be between US$7–9 billion. Many economist and politicians estimate that this construction programme will be one of the key factors which will lie behind boosting the Polish economy.

## ELECTRONICS

The electronic industry in Poland was widely developed during the 1970s and continued its growth in the 1980s. Despite being largely isolated from the Western world during the Communist period, many universities, scientific institutes and research and development departments still managed to keep in touch with the development of modern technologies being introduced all over the world.

One of the strongest benefits of the Polish electronic industry is that it has a well-trained and experienced labour force with many highly qualified engineers and technicians. However, due to financial problems, most of the plants have not been modernised for some years now and as such much of the manufacturing technology used is obsolete – many plants are in the process of restructuring. Most of the electronic manufacturing facilities are located around Warsaw, in the Silesian basin and in northern Poland.

Until the end of the 1980s all Polish electronic factories were owned by the state and controlled by the government. The intention was to make all sectors of Polish industry independent of foreign suppliers. As a result, by the end of the decade Polish factories produced a whole spectrum of electronic products starting from simple parts like resistors, capacitors and transistors through to professional radio and TV equipment, radar, computers etc.

The political and economic changes in Poland have encouraged foreign investors to contribute capital and know-how to the Polish electronics industry, with some of them being very successful, for example Polkolor – Thomson. The last few years have also seen the emergence of a number of thriving private companies (like Curtis Electronics producing TV sets or Optimus making microcomputers).

## ENGINEERING

The engineering sector is one of the largest Polish industrial sectors and is estimated to contribute 23 per cent of Poland's GDP (1993). The sector can be broken down into the following sub-sectors:

|  | % GDP | Number of companies | Employment |
| --- | --- | --- | --- |
| Metal element fabrication | 5.5% | 512 | 163 |
| Machinery | 6.4% | 822 | 308 |
| Transport | 6.2% | 302 | 220 |
| Electrical and electronics | 4.9% | 329 | 137 |

This sector has traditionally been one of the most developed in Polish industry, mainly through:

- good cost competitiveness as compared to other sectors in Poland and direct foreign competitors. This is a result of the relatively high level of technology, low wages and sizeable manufacturing capacity;

- market position. Polish engineering has a large domestic market in which to sell its products and services. It also has access to many foreign markets due to the ability to compete successfully internationally in terms of pricing and quality;

- labour force. The Communist system, in general, encouraged the development of a technically skilled workforce. This trend was especially evident for the engineering sector.

The Polish government has stated in its draft on 'Industrial Policy' for 1993–4 that the engineering sector should be designated as having 'priority needs', as many other industrial sectors have a natural interdependency on this sector. It was also recognised that although the engineering sector had experienced great problems during the Polish economic transformations, it would play a vital and substantial role in the country's future.

There is no doubt that the sector has already started to rebound from the calamitous drop in production in 1990–1, as indicated by a 28 per cent real increase in output in 1992, as compared to 1991, a trend which is believed to continue for the next few years.

Any assessment of the engineering sector should balance the above positive qualities against the sector's poor efficiency, great variation in technological advancement between sub-sectors and companies within the sub-sectors, and poor general management.

## FOOD PROCESSING

Polish food processing is considerably less developed than in Western countries and traditionally the consumption of processed food by Poles has been low. The average rural Pole prefers to buy fresh produce on a daily basis rather than ready-made food products. However, there is a growing demand for processed food products in the larger towns and by the younger generation.

The food processing industry is currently undergoing rapid ownership, organisational, technical and economic transformations – the smaller processing plants are being privatised and the large-scale plants are looking to form joint ventures.

The potential of this sector is reflected by:

- the significant domestic market of nearly 40 million people;
- competitive labour costs and highly skilled production staff;
- large, well-developed, agricultural and livestock sectors, which provide fruits, meat, grains etc;
- significant interest from international food processing companies in entering the Polish market;
- larger demand for efficient food processing machinery. Most of the existing machinery is inefficient, obsolete and in need of modernisation.

The food processing industry is seriously affected by the insufficient quality of packaging materials and machinery, as well as storage and cooling systems. Therefore, storage and packaging would seem to be significant investment opportunities for Western firms.

Ninety-seven per cent of Polish food processing companies are in private hands. There are 1228 companies employing over 50 people, of which 28 per cent employ under 100 people, 24 per cent employ between 101–200 people, 32 per cent employ between 201–500 people and only 1.3 per cent employ over 2001 people.

The meat processing industry is very important for the Polish economy. The total production of meat in 1992 amounted to 1.23 million tonnes, of which 66 per cent was pork, 17 per cent was beef, 16 per cent was poultry and 1 per cent other meat. In addition, there were produced 102,000 tonnes of meat preserves, 1800 tonnes of bacon and 669,000 tonnes of cured meat products, the latter including 84,000 tonnes of cured poultry products.

Unlike the rest of the sector, the Polish meat industry generally utilises modern technology. The biggest problems of this industry seem to be quality control and packaging. State-owned plants usually have quality control laboratories, while private companies quite often do not have such facilities. Although food packaging has improved significantly in recent years, there is still a problem of appropriate packaging machinery and materials, such as sausage casing, films and cans.

The fruit and vegetable processing industry comprises about 500 processing plants, with a predominance of small-scale plants producing under 1000 tonnes of preserves annually. Co-operation between the processing companies and farmers is traditionally based on medium and long-term contracts. The processing industry provides producers with planting material, pesticides, expertise etc.

In 1992 Polish production of frozen fruits amounted to 232,000 tonnes, jams and marmalades 43,000 tonnes, frozen vegetables 110,000 tonnes and canned vegetables 22,100 tonnes.

Traditionally, the Polish dairy industry has been dominated by co-operatives, many of which have been privatised in recent years. Many opportunities are available in the area of product quality control, sanitation and packaging, as well as in developing high value-added dairy products, for example, there is a need to improve the bottling and canning of liquid milk. In 1992 1,234 million litres of milk were produced, 182,000 tonnes of powdered milk and cream, 155,000 tonnes of butter and 286,000 tonnes of cheese of which 165,000 tonnes was cottage cheese.

In the grain processing industry there is a strong requirement for investment in new storage and processing facilities or their modernisation in order to improve quality and reduce wastage. There is, in addition, a need for modern harvesting and grain drying systems, large and smaller scale mills, the construction of grain elevators, metal bins, oil crushing and margarine production packaging machinery etc.

## PAPER

The Polish cellulose paper industry offers some significant advantages to the potential investor:

- large domestic market – population of 40 million with the prospects of considerable growth; annual paper use in Poland is currently about 30 kg per capita – a level far below that of Western Europe (200 kg); other countries in Central Europe (Czech Republic and Hungary) use about 50 kg per capita;

- easy access to raw materials; most of the Polish forests, which cover over 28 per cent of the country's surface area, are young and well suited for processing;

- proximity of large exports markets – the former Soviet Union as well as the Central European countries;
- competitive labour costs, as well as the on-going restructuring of the industry. The companies are reducing their production costs by improving efficiency and increasingly reprocessing waste paper. Currently almost half of the industry's output comes from the private sector;
- a market niche in high quality and specialised paper. At present these are not being manufactured in Poland.

In European terms the Polish paper industry can be regarded as middle ranking, with a production in 1992 of over 1 million tonnes and roughly 600,000 tonnes of cellulose. In 1991, 60 per cent of production was packing (liner, fluting, sack paper, packing paper, cardboard), approximately 30 per cent was writing paper, printing paper and newspapers, and less than 10 per cent was toilet paper.

The industry consists of approximately 60 companies, but over 90 per cent of production comes from the 20 largest factories, of which over half is processed in the four largest plants: Świecie, Kwidzyń, Kostrzyń and Ostrołęka. The majority of main Polish pulp and paper producers have already been privatised, including Kwidzyń SA (80 per cent stake sold to International Paper for US$120 million), Ostroleka, Poznań, Kostrzyń and Cieszyn. However there are still several large Polish producers (Świecie, Kielce, Krapkowice and Skolwin) which are still looking for foreign investors.

## PHARMACEUTICAL

The Polish pharmaceutical sector consists of approximately 200 manufacturers, ranging from large state-owned companies (Polfas) and co-operatives (Herbapols), to a small number of private companies. The sector produces a full range of medicines from traditional herbal confections to modern antibiotics, from the treatment of blood circulatory disorders to veterinary applications. In general Poland is sufficient in the production of basic medicines, mainly antibiotics, but it is the final stage of medicine processing (tablets, pills etc), which has been under-invested, and requires rapid and substantial improvement.

The pharmaceutical sector in Poland has a great deal of potential due to the following factors:

- large domestic market;
- competitive labour costs as well as highly qualified scientific, technical and production staff;

- high quality of pharmaceutical in-bulk, which are manufactured in accordance with international pharmacopoeias (such as *British Pharmacopoeia* or *USA Pharmacopoeia*).

To date only a few foreign companies have started production activities in Poland, such as Solco-Basel, and only very recently has the Eli Lily Corporation signed a letter of intent with Warsaw Biotechnology and Antibiotics Institute to create a joint venture to build a 'greenfield' pharmaceutical factory. However, a large number of forcign pharmaceutical companies have started to sell their medicines through the existing network of state and private pharmacies.

Only two Polish pharmaceutical companies have started the privatisation process: PF Jelfa in Jelenia Góra (IPO) and Kutnowskie Zaklady Farmaceutyczne.

Recently a sector study of the industry was completed by the Boston Consulting Group and Warsaw Consulting Group for the Ministry of Industry and Trade. A restructuring programme for the sector will be shortly prepared on the basis of the final report.

## PROPERTY

Apart from leasing property, foreigners still require the consent of the Minister of Internal Affairs if they intend to buy or have perpetual usufruct of a property (few applications are turned down). However, this problem can be overcome by having a minority shareholding in a company with Polish partners and this company buys the property. Finally the foreign entity buys out the rest of the shares from the Polish partners.

Land prices in Warsaw range between 400 to 1000 USD (city centre) per sq.m. Monthly rental prices in Warsaw are: office space 10–60 USD per sq.m; flats from 10 to 30 USD per sq.m, and residential property up to 10 USD per sq.m. Retail property prices range between 350 USD and 800 USD again depending on location and condition. Prices in the rest of the country are lower by 20 to 60 per cent.

Arable land costs from 130 to 700 USD per hectare, and most arable land is still privately owned. In urban areas, however, more than 50 per cent of land and buildings are still owned by the state.

The progress of reprivatisation (giving property back to the original owners which had been nationalised after World War II) has been slow. The government generally supports this progress, but in many areas it is fraught with difficulties as the property may have already changed hands several times, with the current owner having purchased it in good faith. Therefore, rather than issue a law depriving the current private owner of the property, the government is preparing a draft law which will compensate past owners by awarding them shares of private companies.

# RETAILING

The retailing sector in Poland is currently undergoing rapid development. A large number of shops and restaurants have already become privately operated with consequent tremendous improvements in their image. By the end of 1992 the private sector accounted for 99 per cent, of which 16 per cent were co-operatives.

In the past, there was a very limited access to imported goods, which were mainly sold through the Pewex chain of shops throughout the whole of Poland or by individuals at local bazaars. This situation, however, has changed dramatically with foreign as well as domestic goods being available now almost in every shop.

Some Polish manufacturers have strengthened their brand names, such as the shirt maker Wólczanka and the clothing company Próchnik, by opening their own shops in major towns and the first few major department stores, such as Bogusz Centre or Panorama in Warsaw, have been opened. Private wholesaling is another area of rapid development, covering all kinds of goods from food to consumer products.

Most major car manufacturers have established large networks of well-equipped car dealership outlets and many foreign companies with well-known brand names have also entered the Polish market, such as:

- in fast food sector – McDonald's (already 13 restaurants opened in main cities in Poland), Burger King (7 restaurants already opened), Pepsico through its Pizza Hut, Kentucky Fried Chicken and Taco Bell restaurants;
- in clothing sector – Benetton (already opened 16 shops in Poland's main towns), Levi Strauss & Co;
- in food retailing sector – Billa (Austrian–Polish supermarket chain with 4 supermarkets opened), Hit (German supermarket);
- wholesalers – Makro Cash & Carry (it has just started its operation in Poland and has ambitious future plans);
- in photographic sector – Kodak, Fuji, Agfa (which opened large number of licensed photo processing outlets);
- furniture and department stores – IKEA (4 shops opened).

# SERVICES

In recent years the Polish services sector has become one of the fastest growing industries in the country. This has been fuelled by:

- particularly strong dominance of the private sector in this industry. Even as early as 1980 private business provided nearly 50 per cent of services, growing to 85 per cent by 1990 and still rising;

- the fast development of foreign companies particularly in specialised services such as law, accountancy, medical services, marketing and promotion;
- the previously low priority given to services by the Polish consumer over the past 40 years due to
  - the emphasis was placed on the purchase of goods as the demand for them was never fully satisfied,
  - the poor quality and inadequate structure of services supplied,
  - expectations of services being provided free by the state,
  - the large proportion of the society who had a low income which was insufficient to budget for the purchase of services.

The traditional service consumption structure has changed dramatically over recent years as the number and range of service providers has grown substantially to fill in gaps found in the old service network. This introduction of new types of services created new demand and posed even stronger competition to the state-owned companies – who were often unable to hold on to their position in the market.

In many areas the services sector is still in the early phases of the evolution process and must present some significant investment opportunities for foreign companies. There are, however, certain entry barriers such as:

- increasingly strong competition (domestic and foreign);
- high operating costs (lease, rents) often put excessive pressure on profit margins;
- the relatively high prices of services, recently rising faster than the general price of goods, may reverse current growing demand trends;
- the low priority still given to some types of services in both corporate and consumer sectors, ie Polish companies still do not fully appreciate the importance of marketing, product branding, management information etc.

## SHIPBUILDING AND SHIP REPAIRS

Poland has over 40 years of shipbuilding experience, and together with relatively modern and well-developed production facilities and highly qualified employees, has gained an international reputation for building good quality and competitively priced ships.

The dramatic fall in demand in 1990/1 from the former Soviet Union had a traumatic effect on Polish shipyards. Currently most are going through the process of financial restructuring (Szczecin and Northern Gdańsk shipyard have both signed bank conciliatory agreements), but prospects are bright as

Polish shipyards are making steady inroads into Western markets and demand for new ships is expected to rise internationally as shipowners replace the bulk of their fleets by 2005. In addition, the Polish government is keen to see the continued development of this sector, together with its network of 1500 component suppliers.

The main shipyards are in Gdańsk, Gdynia and Szczecin, and their ships range from specialist research vessels to tankers (widest berth 70 m, maximum 400,000 DWT). These shipyards also undertake overhauls, reconstruction and repairs.

The majority of the shipyards have already been transformed into state-owned joint stock companies and a number have begun to take steps towards privatisation. For instance, part of the equity of Gdańsk shipyard has been given to the employees; there has been debt-to-equity swap under a bank conciliatory agreement at the Northern Gdańsk shipyard; Ustka shipyard is undergoing privatisation through the process of liquidation; Szczecin shipyard has already been privatised.

# TEXTILE AND CLOTHING

Textiles and clothing represent two contrasting models of industrial development in Communist Poland. Textile firms were established on a grand scale, but central planning rendered them inefficient and unprofitable. Clothing firms, on the other hand, tended to remain small and relatively entrepreneurial.

Textile production has a long history in Poland, dating from the eighteenth century. The main textile centre is Lódź and to a lesser extent Częstochowa and Warsaw. The industry received substantial levels of investment under Communism, but the allocation of resources was inconsistent and modern equipment is often found alongside obsolete machinery. According to statistics, however, the textile industry is the most modern industry in Poland with an average of only 38 per cent depreciation on spinning and weaving machinery. None the less, the majority of these machines are of East European origin and technologically lag behind those currently used by Western producers. The textile industry was put under even more pressure when in 1990 cheap supplies of cotton from the Soviet Union suddenly stopped. As a result production dropped by half, severely curtailing competitiveness both within Poland and abroad.

Poland's clothing enterprises, by contrast, continue to thrive. In 1992 the largest investments were made in the clothing sector. Fifty per cent of domestic garment production still comes from state enterprises which are usually multi-plant but also include co-operatives that are far more fragmented and produce more specialised garments. This state sector has recently started to decline due to financial difficulties, greater competition from the private sector, a fall in demand in the domestic market and the state enterprises themselves being privatised. A large number of state enterprises have been privatised or are now being restructured (in terms of organisation and production) in order to be privatised soon, a process which is anticipated to be finished by 1995. This newly created private sector is growing rapidly, for example, three of the largest, formerly state-owned, clothing companies, Próchnik, Wólczanka and Vistula, are quoted on the Warsaw Stock Exchange.

Poland's competitive labour cost position is often used by Western manufacturers in production of garments based on imported fabric and made according to specific designs (Outward Processing Trade). Many of the most expensive garments sold in Paris and London are actually produced by Polish workers as sub-contract tailors. A more attractive form of co-operation between Polish and Western producers, from Poland's point of view, is when the whole production process takes place in Poland, a good example being Levi which has its own factory in Plock producing and selling jeans on the Polish market.

Although the clothing industry is prospering it cannot support the Polish textile sector as long as Polish clothing producers are more interested in production based on fabrics imported by their foreign clients than in buying them locally.

## TOURISM

Located in the centre of Europe, Poland has a huge tourist potential through its immense diversity of natural landscapes and cultural heritage: over 500 km of coastline; numerous rivers; hundreds of lakes, including those in the Great Mazurian Lake District; a variety of mountains, from the alpine Tatras to the smaller lushly forested Bieszczady; picturesque lowland plains and quiet hamlets. Testimony to Poland's history are the old town districts and royal castles of the major cities: Warsaw, Cracow, Gdańsk, Toruń, Wroclaw, Poznań and Lublin, some of which possess special status granted by United Nations Educational, Scientific and Cultural Organisation (USESCO).

The former state tourist organisation Orbis has lost its monopoly, despite having a large chain of hotels, being squeezed by both the many active and rapidly growing domestic private tourist companies, and the multinationals, such as Marriott, Holiday Inn, Novotel, Mercure etc, which have started to set up their own hotels in many Polish cities. Nevertheless opportunities still exist in such areas as:

- three and four-star hotels in city conurbations such as Warsaw, Cracow, Katowice, Gdańsk, or Poznań;
- motorway motels on the existing and planned east/west and north/south highways;

- shopping/leisure and entertainment centres;
- upgrade of Poland's many spa facilities;
- regional conference and exhibition centres;
- holiday camps. As Polish state-owned enterprises face financial difficulties many of them are keen to divest their employee holiday facilities, which are often well situated, but are neglected or in a sorry state of repair.

In the early 1990s, only 1 million beds were available for tourists in Poland. Of a total of some 7 million foreign tourists in 1993, more than 2.5 million came from Western countries. Nevertheless, the estimated tourist revenues of US$1.2 billion accounted for less than three-quarters of the equivalent sum in Hungary.

## TRANSPORTATION SECTOR

Poland's geographical location makes this a particularly important sector which has not yet reached its full potential:

- Poland has a well-developed railway system which is the most intensively used European rail system west of the former Soviet Union;
- There is a well-developed road network, although there are few dual carriageways;
- east–west and north–south trade is well serviced by the important Baltic Sea ports of Gdańsk, Gdynia and Szczecin.

The Polish Ministry of Transportation has announced a major investment programme to upgrade the existing road network with priority given to trade links between East and West European countries. The government is planning to construct 2500 km of highways at an annual rate of at least 100 km. All railway lines in Poland are owned and operated by the Polish State Railways (PKP). Western standard 'Intercity' trains link major Polish cities, while the 'Eurocity' service connects Warsaw with other European capitals.

Transportation comes fourth position, in terms of value of assets, behind manufacturing industry, agriculture and housing sectors. However, transportation's share of GDP is only 3.9 per cent, which is far below West European standards.

Generally the Polish transportation system requires substantial capital investment in order to be brought up to EC standards, especially in the areas of technology and quality of service. Although current demands are met, there is a real fear that it is not prepared for the future development of the Polish economy. Foreign investors consider Polish transport to be one of the serious obstacles (along with telecommunications and banking) in discouraging investment in Poland. Therefore it is now one of the most important investment targets for the government.

Poland is a manufacturer of average quality rolling stock which it has traditionally exported to Eastern Europe. Negotiations are currently taking place with Western manufacturers to inject the necessary capital and technology to raise this sector's competitiveness in terms of costs and quality to also be able to export to Western markets.

## Appendix 2

# Economic Assistance

### EUROPEAN BANK FOR RECONSTRUCTION AND DEVELOPMENT

The European Bank for Reconstruction and Development (EBRD) is an international financial institution (IFI),which was established to finance both private and public sector projects in Central and Eastern Europe exclusively, including the former Soviet Union. The Bank was founded in April 1991 by 39 countries, the European Community and the European Investment Bank, with an initial subscribed equity capital of ECU 10 billion and a mandate to: 'foster the transition process towards open market-oriented economies and to promote private and entrepreneurial initiative in the Central and Eastern European countries...' The Bank has a strong private sector focus but remains unique among many other financial institutions in that it is capable of financing both private and public sector projects. A wide variety of financial instruments are offered by the Bank including loans, equity, guarantees and underwriting.

As of 30 June 1994, the EBRD had approved approximately ECU 752 million of direct investment in 34 projects in Poland. Thirty private sector projects, accounting for around 70 per cent of the committed total, are in a variety of commercial sectors, including commercial banking, venture capital funds, food processing, consumer products, automotive products, telecommunications, power generation, paper manufacture, printing and property. The other four state sector loans, totalling ECU 239 million, are in the telecommunications, heating and housing sectors.

Within Poland, the EBRD has no specific sector or geographic focus, other than that required for prudent investment portfolio management. All varieties of proposals are being considered, ranging from financing capital expenditure for existing companies or greenfield construction of new manufacturing sites, to direct equity investments. All proposals are evaluated according to commercial criteria, similar to those that would be used by any prudent financial institution in similar transactions.

The Bank's future focus in Poland will essentially be similar to that of the region as a whole; it will continue to promote the development of a strong private sector, strengthen public infrastructure and catalyse financial sector reform within Poland.

In the private sector, the emphasis of the Bank's activities is expected to move away from the foreign sponsored joint ventures that have been the traditional clients in the past, towards financing projects and companies with majority domestic ownership or focus. In addition, the Bank will concentrate on further developing its links with financial intermediaries that are capable of channelling funds into the smaller and medium-sized companies. The Bank is actively working upon a number of venture capital and equity fund projects, including mechanisms for supporting the proposed mass privatisation programme.

## THE WORLD BANK

The World Bank, the largest global aid agency, began lending to Poland as recently as 1990 with the purpose of contributing to the country's transformation to a market-based economy.

At the start of 1994 lending to Poland had totalled more than $2.5 billion, with a further $2 billion of projected loans still in the pipeline. Amongst early loans was a structural adjustment loan targeted at encouraging private sector enterprise, the reform of the private sector, and the provision of assistance in the social sector.

More recently, sectors that have benefited from World Bank financing have included industry, telecommunications, transport, agriculture and health. Amongst loans that are expected to be approved shortly, energy and education will receive assistance.

As with most aid agencies, the World Bank will only contribute a portion – usually no more than 40 per cent – of the required financing for a given project. However, the Bank's support for a project will often provide comfort for other investors and lead to co-financing from other aid agencies and commercial banks.

Another important factor of many World Bank loans is that they include lines of credit that are administered through the major Polish commercial banks. Western companies and individuals seeking to exploit business opportunities arising from World Bank assistance should, in the first instance, contact these institutions in order to evaluate the possibilities.

## THE INTERNATIONAL FINANCE CORPORATION

The International Finance Corporation (IFC) is an affiliate of the World Bank and the largest source of direct project financing in developing countries. The IFC only operates in ventures that are mainly privately sponsored. In its last financial year to June 1994, the IFC approved worldwide financing of US$4.3 billion.

The IFC has been active in Poland since 1987. It approved its first investment in 1988 and opened a resident mission in 1990. After providing advisory assistance to the Polish government in the early days of the transformation, the IFC developed a strong activity in project finance, advisory services and capital market development.

Project financing is the IFC's largest area of activity in Poland. To date over $350 million in equity and loans has supported 30 projects, including 14 smaller ones through a credit line. The largest of these projects has seen some $67 million invested in a joint venture to privatise a glass company, Huta Sandomierz, and to build the first float glass plant in Poland at a total project cost of $170 million.

The IFC has also supported the restructuring of capital markets in Poland, encouraged the provision of corporate financial services, and has set up and is managing the Polish Business Advisory Service (PBAS).

## PHARE – THE NEW FRAMEWORK

This indicative programme sets out the approach and overall framework for co-operation under the PHARE programme over the period 1993 to 1995.

PHARE is a major G-24 assistance programme to Eastern Europe, co-ordinated by the EC Commission. The allocation for the 1993 programme in Hungary was ECU 225 million.

This amount is conditional on, amongst others, continuing progress with economic reforms and the effective implementation of ongoing PHARE programmes. Particular importance is attached to the government's commitment to the privatisation process, keeping the budget deficit within acceptable limits and carrying on reforms concerned with 'social insurance' expenditure.

The Polish government has decided that PHARE assistance over the medium term should focus on the following core areas:

- infrastructure;
- private sector development;
- public sector reform; *and*
- human resources development.

In these core areas emphasis in 1993 has been laid on strategic support for the following key sectors: transport, industry, customs and education. Other key sectors such as social security are being prepared for substantial allocations within the 1993–1995 time frame.

Infrastructural shortcomings in transport, postal services and telecommunications are significantly slowing down the reform process. In previous years, PHARE has provided path finding support in both transport and telecommunications. Building on the information acquired, the main efforts over the next three years will be devoted to transportation problems.

To develop the private sector, PHARE will emphasise its support to the privatisation programme. Support will be targeted toward the Agencies carrying out the process, the banking sector and individual enterprises. Additional support will be provided to the Ministry of Privatisation to help it attract foreign investment. The privatisation programme currently concentrates on the agricultural, financial and industrial sectors. Support in this area will also be provided to investment promotion measures, SRP and the STRUDER programme (a PHARE regional development programme).

The public sector has been receiving PHARE support for the transformation of its administrative structures. The foundations have been prepared for the final stage of reform in the Trade Infrastructure (Customs) sector, where the essential technological and logistical infrastructure now needs to be provided. The public sector core area will handle problems in customs, statistics and land information as well.

The Human Resources core area (social security, health and education) has fundamentally more complex and far reaching issues to address than other core areas. Essential ground work is still being carried out in preparation for future programmes in most sectors. In education, a substantial reform programme spanning over the next three years is to begin this year. PHARE will also handle problems in science and technology, labour market reform, social security and health.

## *Past Performance*

A detailed review indicates that over the period 1990 to 1992, PHARE support has been made available to address (to a greater or lesser extent) each of the major economic and structural components which needed to undergo transformation in the change from a centrally planned to a market economy.

Since a significant part of the support is provided for the transformation and setting up of new structures, a process requiring varied legislative and policy formulations, the disbursement for such programmes takes place over a long time scale. Their visible impact can thus be either small or not very visible: for example, the programme supporting the introduction and extension of the income tax base has led to a significant increase in the number of tax payers – an outstanding, yet almost invisible, achievement.

Many programmes are performing satisfactorily and may require only modest further funding. Some programmes, for example in the area of trade infrastructure, have completed their initial foundation-laying activities and have prepared the way for larger scale activities.

Total commitment to Poland so far amounts to 577.8 million ECU (180 million ECU in 1990, 197 million ECU in 1991 and 200 million ECU in 1992). Contracting rates so far are 70.2 per cent for 1990 funds; 24.3 per cent for 1991 funds and 13.3 per cent for 1992 funds[1].

# KNOW HOW FUND

The UK's Know How Fund (KHF) programme in Poland is its largest in Central Europe. Some £45 million of the £50 million pledged in 1989 will have been spent by the end of the financial year 1994/95. Priority areas for assistance include banking/financial services, privatisation, energy (especially energy efficiency), industrial restructuring, management development and employment. Consideration is also being given to assistance in the area of EU integration.

In addition to the KHF, the UK has committed £15 million to the Agricultural Development Fund which will have spent around £6 million by the end of 1994. The UK has also reallocated the returned UK contribution to the Polish Stabilisation Fund ($100 million) to mutually agreed development projects.

## *Know How Fund Projects*

*Mass privatisation*
Up to the end of the financial year 1993/94, the UK has spent around £5 million in support of the mass privatisation programme, in the form of technical assistance to help establish capital markets and advise on foreign investment applications.

*Management and accountancy*
Accountancy training has been allocated £4.3 million to facilitate the introduction of market-economy accounting into the curricula of the Polish higher education and vocational training institutions, to facilitate the training of trainers. In addition, £5 million has been set aside for the establishment of four regional management centres (RMCs) in Gdansk, Lodz, Poznan and Lublin. The RMCs will provide high quality training in an increasing competitive market.

*Industry*
The Polish industrial sector will undergo large scale structural change over the next few years and there will be need for massive investment. Plans for IBRD investment are already well advanced. Much of the task of working up programmes in the industrial sector has been delegated to the United Nations Industrial Development Organisation (UNIDO), who vet proposals to the KHF. UNIDO are currently implementing studies for the restructuring of nine Polish companies.

---

[1] stand in April 1993

*Banking and financial services*

The aim is to promote an efficient financial infrastructure which must first be fundamentally re-orientated. The main KHF efforts are directed at company privatisation and help in introducing systems to establish capital markets and encourage foreign investment. Importance will also be given to commercial banking. One project in support of banking training at Katowice Banking School (about £2 million) aims to develop a variety of courses which will provide the training necessary to support the reforms now underway in the banking sector.

*English language training*

A high priority for KHF funding is the training of teachers of English for specialised purposes, ie business English, English for management. Two key programmes are Polish access to English for management (PACE) and the English for management scheme (EMAS). A further project (TRAIL) worth £1.8 million has recently been approved, this builds on our existing programmes of training and academic links.

*Local government*

A programme of training, based at Leicester Polytechnic, was undertaken in 1990/91. This programme had the twin aims of providing Polish councillors with exposure to local government practices, procedures and problems in England, and to provide education for selected trainers and instructors on how to deliver training packages within Poland. This was followed by the local government assistance programme (around £2 million) which has the aim of strengthening the institutional and management capacity of local authorities across Poland.

*Energy*

In the energy sector the KHF has financed four major consultancies to support economic re-structuring of key energy sectors; specifically oil and gas, electricity, lignite and district heating and the hard coal sector. We have also supported a related study on energy pricing.

*Investment support*

Some £2.5 million has been offered so far to British firms seeking investment in Poland. Eighty-one grants have been awarded under the KHF pre-investment feasibility studies (PIFS) scheme, and 30 firms have applied successfully for training grants under the training for investment personnel scheme (TIPS).

*Manager attachments*

The KHF is also financing a successful British Council/CBI-administered programme enabling Polish managers to spend three or four week attachments with UK companies. Over 180 managers have come since 1990 with a further 120 attachments planned over the two years to July 1996.

## Agricultural Development Fund Projects

The Agricultural Development Fund is financing a number of projects in support of the World Bank's agricultural sector adjustment loan (ASAL). The initial commitment was for £6 million to be spent over two years in support of eight projects (now being implemented). The latest project approved is the operational audit of the Polish agency for agricultural markets, which is of central importance in determining whether the Poles can draw down the second tranche of the World Bank loan.

## Stabilisation Fund Projects

In 1989 the UK and other donors set up a Polish Stabilisation Fund (PSF); the UK's contribution to this fund was $100 million. The fund was terminated in 1993 and the UK contribution has been recycled for mutually agreed development projects in Poland. The principal amount ($75 million) has been committed to the Polish Bank privatisation fund. A further $8 million has been committed to providing technical assistance to partner banks, to help with the problem of resolving bad debts. Seventeen million dollars has also been committed to a new project to assist with enterprise restructuring with partner banks. In addition, the interest on the original PSF contribution has been committed to a new project to assist the development of small and medium sized enterprises (the Polish British Enterprise Project).

*Appendix 3*

# Sources of Further Information

## THE CONTRIBUTORS

**BMF International Ltd**
Al. Jerozolimskie 53
00-950 Warsaw
Tel: (48) 2 628 44 71
Fax: (48) 2 628 33 59
Contact: Konrad Urbanski

**Nabarro Nathanson**
ul. Senatorska 12
00-082 Warsaw
Tel: (48) 22 27 61 44
Fax: (48) 22 27 48 38
Contact: Michael Davies

**RZB**
36-38 Botolph Lane
London EC3R 8DE
Tel: (44) 71 929 2288
Fax: (44) 71 220 7560
Contact: Michael Oldfield –
   Manager, Credit and Marketing

**Deloitte & Touche
Warsaw**
ul. Grzybowska 80/82
00-844 Warsaw
Tel: (48) 2 661 53 00
Fax: (48) 2 661 53 50
Contact: Andrzej Kolinski, Jan
   Maciejewicz, George Szyman,
   Michael Barrington

**Deloitte Touche Tohmatsu
International**
Hill House
1 Little New Street
London EC4A 3TR
Tel: (44) 71 9365 30 00
Fax: (44) 71 583 85 17
Contact: Terry M Browne –
   European Tax Director

**Deloitte & Touche
Eastern Europe**
185 Avenue Charles-de Gaulle
92200 Neuilly sur Seine
France
Tel: (33) 1 40 99 28 00
Fax: (33) 1 40 88 29 29
Contact: J Thomas Presby – Chief
   Executive Officer

**Saatchi & Saatchi Advertising**
ul. Moliera 6
00-076 Warsaw
Tel: (48) 22 269 491
Fax: (48) 22 263 803
Contact: Brian Dunnion – Chief
   Executive Officer

**Gerald Eve International**
Wilcza 46
00-679 Warsaw
Tel: (48) 2 621 0692
Fax: (48) 2 625 2988
Contact: Michael Roskelly

**Jakubowski CTAD**
43 Clifton Road
Cambridge CB1 4FB
Tel: 0223 312 704
Fax: 0223 412 275
Contact: Leszek Jakubowski – Director

**GJW Government Relations**
64 Clapham High Road
London SW9 0JJ
Tel: (44) 71 582 3119
Fax: (44) 71 735 9561
Contact: Andrew Ellis or Luisa Kolodziejuk

**British Chamber of Commerce Poland**
27a Krolewska
00-060 Warsaw
Tel: (48) 22 27 72 82 (x1233)
Fax: (48) 22 27 69 15 (x1235)
Contact: Barbara Stachowiak

**Matthew Cadbury** – Regional Development Director, Confectionery
Cadbury Schweppes plc
25 Berkeley Square
London W1X 6HT
Tel: 071 409 1313
Fax: 071 830 5213

**Keith Beckett** – Technical Director, Europe
Pilkington Europe SA
Pilkington Technology Centre
Hall Lane
Lathom
Ormskirk L40 5UF
Tel: 0695 50000
Fax: 0695 54809

**Elektrim-Towarzystwo Handlowe SA**
ul. Tytusa Chałubińskiego 8
PO Box 638; 00-50 Warszawa
Tel: 48·(3912) 02 27 (Komertel)
      48 (22) 30 10 00
      48 (22) 30 09 06
      48 (22) 30 21 65
Fax: 48 (22) 30 08 41-2
Contact: Andrzej Skowtanski – President, Management Board

**Unicorn Poland Sp z o.o.**
ul. DLUGA 27
00-238 Warsaw
Tel: 010 48 22 313 121/314620
Fax: 010 48 2 635 8250
Contact: Wojciech Kossakowski, Managing Director

**Unicorn Ltd**
213 Parkway House
Sheen Lane
London SW14 8LS
Tel: 081 876 5805
Fax:
Contact: Stanislav Staruch

# UNITED KINGDOM

**Export Promoter, Poland**
DTI
Kingsgate House
66-74 Victoria Street
London SW1E 6SW
Tel: 44 (71) 215 8190
Fax: 44 (71) 215 2866
Contact: John Evans

**Confederation of British Industry**
Centre Point
103 New Oxford Street
London WC1A 1DU
Tel: 44 (71) 379 7400
Fax: 44 (71) 836 1972
Contact: Pauline Shearman – Head of Central and East European Department, International Affairs Directorate

**Department of Trade and Industry**
Poland Desk
Kingsgate House
66-74 Victoria Street
London SW1E 6SW
Tel: 44 (71) 215 5256
Fax: 44 (71) 215 4743
Contact: Siobhan Menary

**Department of Trade and Industry**
Export Market Information Centre (EMIC)
Ashdown House
125 Victoria Street
London SW1E 6RB
Tel: 44 (71) 215 5444
Fax: 44 (71) 215 4231

**Department of Trade and Industry**
World Aid Section
Room 291
Ashdown House
123 Victoria Street
London SW1E 6RB
Tel: 44 (71) 215 6210/6089
Fax: 44 (71) 215 6535

**East European Trade Council**
10 Westminster Palace Gardens
Artillery Road
London SW1P 1RL
Tel: 44 (71) 222 7622
Fax: 44 (71) 222 5359
Contact: J A McNeish – Director

**Embassy of the Republic of Poland**
Commercial Section
15 Devonshire Street
London W1N 2AR
Tel: 44 (71) 580 7472
Fax: 44 (71) 323 0195
Contact: Dr Romuald Szuniewicz – Commercial Counsellor

**Polish Trade and Commercial Centre Ltd**
33 Davies Street
Mayfair
London W1Y 1FN
Tel: 44 (71) 492 1599
Fax: 44 (71) 493 1581

**The Polish Enterprise Centre**
POSK
238-246 King Street
London W6 0RF
Tel: (44) 81 563 7311
Fax: (44) 81 563 7299
Contact: Adam Robinski

# POLAND

## General

**British Embassy**
Warsaw Corporate Centre
Second Floor
ul. Emilii Plater 28
Warsaw
Tel: 010 482 625 3030
Fax: 010 482 625 3472
Contact: Mr Anthony Gooch – First Secretary (Commercial)

**British Chamber of Commerce in Poland**
27A Krolewska Street (Suite 371)
00-060 Warsaw
Tel: 010 4822 277 282 (x 1233)
Fax: 010 4822 277 282 (x 1235)
Contact: Barbara Stachowiak

**Centre for International Economic and Scientific Cooperation**
(CIESC)
272B Piotrkowska St
30-361 Lodz
Tel: 010 4842 819 666
Fax: 010 4842 336 892
Contact: Janusz Golygowski

**Chamber of Industry and Trade for Foreign Investors**
ul. Krakowskie Przedmiescie 47/51
00-071 Warsaw
Fax: 010 482 268 593

**Polish Chamber of Commerce**
ul. Trebacka 4
00-950 Warsaw
Tel: 010 48 22 274 741
Fax: 010 48 22 274 673
Contact: Zaneta Berus

**State Agency for Foreign Investment**
Al Roz 2
00-559 Warsaw
Tel: 010 482 2295 717
Fax: 010 482 621 8427
Contact: Marek Gorski, President

**Industrial Development Agency**
ul. Wspolna 4
00-926 Warsaw
Tel: 010 482 621 6570
Fax: 010 482 628 2363
Contact: Arkadiusz Krezel, President

**'Poland Now' Foundation**
ul. Krucza 38/42
00-512 Warsaw
Tel: 010 482 628 2882
Fax: 010 482 621 9761
Contact: Bogdan Chojna, President

**The Central Planning Office**
pl. Trzech Krzyzy 5
00-507 Warsaw
Tel: 010 482 693 5000
Fax: 010 482 628 5754/215 5164

**Central Bank**
ul. Swietokrzyska 11/21
00-950 Warsaw
Tel: 010 482 200 321

**Bank Handlowy w Warszawie SA**
ul. T Chalubinskiego 8
00-950 Warsaw
Tel: 010 482 300 300
Fax: 010 482 300 113

**The Main Statistical Office (Główny Urząd Statystyczny)**
Al Niepodległości 208
00-925 Warszawa
Tel: 48 (22) 25 24 31
      48 (22) 25 32 41

**Polish Press Agency (Polska Agencja Prasowa)**
Al. Jerozolimskie 7
Warszawa
Tel: 48 (2) 628 00 01
   48 (22)21 34 39

**The National Library (Biblioteka Narodowa)**
Al. Niepodległości 213
00-925 Warszawa
Tel: 48 (22) 25 92 70

**The Warsaw School of Economics (Szkoła Główna Handlowa)**
Al. Niepodległości 162
00-925 Warszawa
Tel: 48 (22) 49 12 51
   48 (22) 48 50 61
   48 (22) 49 50 48 (library)

**Business Foundation**
ul. Krucza 38/42
00-512 Warszawa
Tel: 48 (3912) 00 77
   48 (2) 628 28 82
   48 (22) 21 99 93
Fax: 48 (22) 21 97 61

**Kompass Poland Ltd**
ul. Jasna 1
00-013 Warszawa
Tel: 48 (22) 27 26 53 (x Kompass)
   48 (22) 26 72 21 (x Kompass)
Fax: 48 (22) 27 28 18

**Patent Office**
Al. Niepodleglosci 188/192
00-669 Warsaw
Tel: 010 482 258 001
Fax: 010 482 250 581

**Central Board of Customs**
ul. Swietokrzyska 12
00-916 Warsaw
Tel: 010 482 268 465
Fax: 010 482 273 427

**President of the Board of Customs**
pl. Powstancow 1
Tel: 010 482 218 427

*Ministries*

**Ministry of Agriculture and Food Economy (MAFE)**
Department of Foreign and Economic Cooperation
ul. Wspolna 30
00-930 Warsaw
Tel: 010 482 623 2073/2005
Fax: 010 482 623 2750/2751
Contact: Eugeniusz Tyszkowski

**Ministry of Foreign Economic Relations**
Promotion Department
Pl Trzech Krzyzy 5
00-950 Warsaw
Tel: 010 482 628 3988
Fax: 010 482 625 5159
Contact: Wanda Samborska – Director

**Ministry of Privatisation**
Foreign Cooperation Department
ul. Krucza 36
00-525 Warsaw
Tel: 010 482 628 6232
Fax: 010 482 621 2550
Contact: Michael Mrozek – Director

**Ministry of Industry and Trade**
Foreign Cooperation Department
ul. Wspolna 4
00-926 Warsaw
Tel: 010 482 628 2141
Fax: 010 482 621 2550
Contact: Janusz Zgorzynski – Director

**Ministry of Finance**
ul. Swietokrzyska 12
00-916 Warsaw
Tel: 010 482 694 5555

**Ministry of Regional Planning and Construction**
ul. Wspolna 2
00-505 Warsaw
Tel: 010 482 210 351
Fax: 010 482 628 5887

**Ministry of Communications**
pl. Malachowskiego 2
00-063 Warsaw
Tel: 010 482 261 411
Fax: 010 482 264 840

**Ministry of Transport and Maritime Economy**
ul. Chalubinskiego 4/6
Tel: 010 482 244 000

**Ministry of Environmental Protection, Natural Resources and Forestry**
ul. Wawelska 52/54
02-067 Warsaw
Tel: 010 482 250 001 to 9
Fax: 010 482 253 335/972

## ECONOMIC ASSISTANCE

**PHARE Information Office**
AN 88 1/26
EC Commission
200 rue de la Loi
B-1049 Brussels
Tel: 010 (32) 2 299 1356/1400
Fax: 010 (32) 2 299 1777
Contact: Tom Glaser

**PHARE (National Co-ordination Office)**
Office For Foreign Assistance
Council of Ministers
Al. Vjaz dowskie 9
00-950 Warsaw
Tel: 00 (48) 2 628 8630
Fax: (48) 22 29 28 88
Contact: Pawel Samechi – Director General

**Know-How Fund**
Joint Assistance Unit
Foreign and Commonwealth Office
Old Admiralty Building
London SW1A 2AF
Tel: 44 (71) 210 0005
Fax: 44 (71) 210 0010
Contact: Julian Ebsworth

**Joint Industrial and Commercial Attachments Programme**
Industrial Training Unit
The British Council
10 Spring Gardens
London SW1A 2BN
Tel: 44 (71) 389 4076
Fax: 44 (71) 389 4090
Contact: John Moore

**European Bank for Reconstruction and Development**
One Exchange Square
London EC2A 2EH
Tel: 44 (71) 338 6665
Fax: 44 (71) 338 7199
Contact: Charles Wrangham

**European Bank for Reconstruction and Development (Poland)**
Al. Jerozolimskie 65/79
00-697 Warsaw
Tel: 010 482 630 7275
Fax: 010 482 630 6551
Contact: Yves Fortin

**The World Bank**
Intraco Building
ul. Stawki 2
00-193 Warsaw
Tel: 010 482 635 0553
Fax: 010 482 635 9857
Contact: Paul Knotter, resident representative

**International Monetary Fund**
ul. Stawki 2
00-193 Warsaw
Tel: 010 482 635 8506/8505
Fax: 010 482 635 9857

**The International Finance Corporation**
ul. Emilii Plater-28
00-688 Warsaw
Tel: 010 482 630 3444
Fax: 010 482 630 3445
Contact: Hugh Stevenson

# Index

accounting 83–7
  audit requirements 86–7
  policies 84–6
    capitalisation of interest 85–6
    deferred taxation 86
    depreciation 84–5
    foreign exchange 86
    intangibles 85
    inventory valuation 86
    leased assets 85
    R&D costs 85
    revaluation of assets 85
  practices 84
  reporting requirements 83–4
advertising 142–3
agencies/distributorships 133–4
agriculture 197–8
  agricultural tax 93
  Know How Fund projects 219–20
airports 123
area permits 71–2
assets 66, 85
  asset/liability management 66
  intangibles 85
  leased 85
  revaluation of 85
audiovisual works/equipment 139, 152
audit requirements 86–7
automotive industry 198–9

banking 53–5
  bank loans 170
  banking law 54
  Central Bank 53

clearing system 54
deposit insurance 55
EBRD 35, 159, 160, 161, 215–16
foreign exchange market 55
interbank market 54
interest rates 55
money market 55
Polish Development Bank (PDB) 81, 161
reform of Polish system 53–4
World Bank 124, 216
BMF International Ltd 19–24, 39–42, 43–6, 57–62, 63–9, 77–82, 117–21, 197–214
bonded warehouses 129
bonds 80–1
  corporate 81
  government 80–1
  municipal 81
brewing industry 197–8
British Chamber of Commerce in Poland 123–6
broking companies 54, 78–9
building/development controls 98–9
business context 17–46
  business culture 39–42
    *introduction* 39
    company's role in community 39–40
    Polish workforce 40
    practicalities 41–2
    work ethic 40–1
  capital markets 77–82
    bonds 80–1
    equities 77–9

money matters 81–2
economic reform 25–7
employment law 105–12
  *introduction* 105
  contract of employment 105–6
  foreign employees 111
  individual's rights 109–10
  redundancy 108–9
  relating to directors 110
  social security 112
  termination of contracts 106–8
  trade unions 110
  working hours/time off 111
environment 117–21
  *introduction* 117–18
  foreign investor 118–21
fiscal regime 89–93
  agricultural tax 93
  corporate income tax 90
  individual income tax 90–1
  real property tax 92–3
  social insurance contributions (ZUS) 92
  stamp duty 9
  tax authorities 89–90
  VAT and excise tax 91–2
foreign investment 71–5
  *introduction* 71
  approvals 71–3
  direct 58
  and the environment 118–21
  protection of foreign investors 73–4
  repatriation of profits 74–5
  representative offices 75
  sources of capital 74
labour market 113–15
legal framework 33–7
  *introduction* 33
  European trade 36
  privatisation 34–6
  property 33–4
  *conclusion* 36–7
market intelligence 43–6
  company directors 45
  foreign trade companies 44
  Infodata 46
  institutes 45
  libraries 45
  local authorities 45

Main Statistical Office (GUS) 43–4
  ministries 44
  the press 44–5
  specialised companies 44
  State Agency for Foreign Investment (PAIZ) 43
Poland and its potential 19–24
  *introduction* 19
  establishing a free market economy 20–2
  foreign investment 22–4
  history 20–1
political transformation 29–32
  back to power 30–2
  the great divide 19–30
privatisation 57–62
  capital 57, 59–60
  direct foreign investment 58
  liquidation of SOE 58
  management/employee buy-outs 57–8
  mass program 58, 60–2
  restructuring 62
  winding-up 57
property 33–4, 95–103
  land acquisition permits 73
  real estate 100–3
  regulations 95–100
  tax 92–3
restructuring state enterprises 63–9
  *introduction* 63
  financial restructuring 65–6
  historical background 63–5
  operational restructuring 67
  the restructuring programme 67–9
utilities 123–6
  *introduction* 123
  energy 123–4
  roads/ports 124–5
  telecommunications 125–6
valuation and accounting 83–7
  accounting policies 84–6
  accounting practices 84
  audit requirements 86–7
  reporting requirements 83–4
business infrastructure 47–126
  banking 53–5
    banking law 54
    Central Bank 53

Index   233

 clearing system 54
 deposit insurance 55
 foreign exchange market 55
 interbank market 54
 interest rates 55
 money market 55
 reform of Polish system 53–4
foreign exchange 49–51
 *introduction* 49
 exchange controls 50
 external transactions 50
 internal transactions 50
 remittance of profits 51
Business Support Centres 114

Cadbury Schweppes 187–9
capital 77–82
 capitalisation of interest 85–6
 management 66
 markets 77–82
  bonds 80–1
  equities 77–9
  money matters 81–2
 privatisation 57, 59–60
 sources of 74
case studies 177–93
 Cadbury Schweppes 187–9
 Elektrim 179–82
 Pilkington 183–5
 Unicorn Poland 191–3
Central Bank 53
Central European Free Trade Agreement (CEFTA) 21
certificates of deposit 81
chemical industry 136, 200–1
clearing system, bank 54
clothing sector 134, 209
coal industry 121, 201–2
community, local 39–40
company directors 45
company formation 173–6
 *introduction* 173
 joint stock companies 174–6
 limited liability companies 173–4
computer software 152, 191–3
conferences, trade 146
construction industry 202–3
contracts 105–8
 of employment 105–6

 termination 106–8
copyright 151–2
 audiovisual works 152
 computer software 152
 criminal liability 152
 nature of 151–2
 related rights 151
corporate bonds 81
corporate income tax 90
culture, business 39–42
 *introduction* 39
 company's role in community 39–40
 Polish workforce 40
 practicalities 41–2
 work ethic 40–1
customs and excise 128–32
 administration/procedure 130–1
 duties 91–2
 duties/international agreements 129–30
 duty free zones/bonded warehouses 131
 excise tax 29–30
 exemptions 131

deferred taxation 86
Deloitte & Touche, Warsaw 83–7, 89–93
deposit insurance 55
depreciation, accounting for 84–5
development controls 98–9
directors, company 110
distribution 139–41
 distributorships 133–4
duty free zones/bonded warehouses 131

*East-West Joint Ventures* (UN) 134
ECGD 148–9
economic assistance 215–21
 contacts 216
 European Bank for Reconstruction and Development (EBRD) 215–16
 International Finance Corporation (IFC) 216–17
 Know How Fund 219–21
 PHARE - the new framework 217–18
 sources of information 228
 World Bank 216
economic reform 25–7
electronics industry 203–4
Elektrim 179–82

background 179
early 1990s 179–80
the future 181
privatisation 182
employment law 105–12
*introduction* 105
contract of employment 105–6
foreign employees 111
individual's rights 109–10
redundancy 108–9
general 108
procedure 108–9
severance pay 109
relating to directors 110
social security 112
termination of contracts 106–8
periods of notice 106
procedure 107
restrictions 107
unlawful upon notice 107
unlawful without notice 108
without notice 107–8
trade unions 110
working hours/time off 111
energy 121–2
engineering industry 202–3
environment 117–21
*introduction* 117–18
foreign investor 118–21
acquisition 120–21
greenfield sites 119
operational issues 120
equities market 77–9, 162
broking companies 78–9
capital raising 79
investment funds 79
listing requirements 78
regulatory framework 77
European Bank for Reconstruction and Development (EBRD) 35, 159, 160, 161, 215–16
European trade 36
exchange controls 50
excise duties *see* customs and excise
expropriation of land 100
external transactions 50

fairs, trade 146
finance, project *see* project finance

finance, trade *see* trade finance
financial restructuring 65–6
asset/liability management 66
capital management 66
lack of information 66
working capital 66
fiscal regime 89–93
agricultural tax 93
corporate income tax 90
individual income tax 90–1
real property tax 92–3
social insurance contributions (ZUS) 92
stamp duty 93
tax authorities 89–90
VAT and excise tax 91–2
food processing industry 134, 205–6
foreign employees 111
foreign exchange 49–51, 54
*introduction* 49
accounting policies 86
exchange controls 50
external transactions 50
internal transactions 50
market 55
remittance of profits 51
foreign investment 22–4, 71–5
*introduction* 71
approvals 71–3
acquisition of land 73
shares in existing companies 72
specific permits 72–3
strategic area permits 71–2
direct 58
and the environment 117–21
acquisition 120–21
greenfield sites 119
operational issues 120
protection of foreign investors 73–4
repatriation of profits 74–5
representative offices 75
sources of capital 74
foreign trade companies 44
franchising 134–5

Gerald Eve International 95–103
GJW Government Relations 29–32
government bonds 80–1
greenfield sites 119
GUS *see* Main Statistical Office

history of Poland 20-1
holidays 111
hotel markets 102

income tax 90-1
industrial designs 157-8
industrial markets 101-2
Infodata 46
information 223-9
  lack of company 66, 67
  sources of 43-6, 223-9
    contributors 223-4
    economic assistance 228-9
    Poland 226-8
    United Kingdom 225
infrastructure, business *see* business infrastructure
institutes 45
intangibles, accounting for 85
intellectual property 151-8
  *introduction* 151
  copyright 151-2
    audiovisual works 152
    computer software 152
    criminal liability 152
    nature of 151-2
    related rights 152
  industrial designs/utility models/semiconductors 157-8
  patents 152-5
    *introduction* 152
    compulsory licensing 154-5
    duration 154
    enforcing rights 155
    international relations 152-3
    inventions created during employment 154
    obtaining rights 153-4
    scope of coverage 153
  trade marks 155-7
    assignment/licensing 156-7
    cancellation 157
    duration 156
    enforcement 157
    international agreements 155
    legislation 155
    protection of foreign marks 155
    registration of 156
    scope of coverage 155-6

interbank market 54, 81-2
internal transactions 50
International Finance Corporation (IFC) 216-17
International Monetary Fund (IMF) 26
inventory valuation 86
investment, foreign 163-72
  equities investment funds 79
  finance 169-72
    bank loans 170
    public debt 170-1
    stock issues 169-70
    tax incentives 171-2
  investment strategy 163-7

Jakubowski CTAD Ltd 113-15

KIR *see* National Clearing House
Know How Fund 219-21
  agricultural projects 221
  projects 219-20
  stabilisation projects 221

labour market 113-15
land 34
  acquisition permits 73
  registry 97-8
leased assets 34, 85, 96-7
legislation
  banking law 54
  employment law 105-12
    *introduction* 105
    contract of employment 105-6
    foreign employees 111
    individual's rights 109-10
    redundancy 108-9
    relating to directors 110
    social security 112
    termination of contracts 106-8
    trade unions 110
    working hours/time off 111
  financial restructuring 65-6
  legal framework 33-7
    *introduction* 33
    European trade 36
    privatisation 34-6
    property 33-4
    *conclusion* 36-7

National Investment Funds (NIF) Law (1993) 61–2
  property 95–103
    acquisition/leasing by foreigners 98
    building/development controls 98–9
    expropriation 100
    interests in land 96–7
    land registry 97–8
    restitution 100
    tax 100
  trade marks 155–6
liability management 66
libraries 45

Main Statistical Office (GUS) 43–4
management/employee buy-outs 57–8
market economy, establishing a free 20–2
market intelligence 43–6
  company directors 45
  foreign trade companies 44
  Infodata 46
  institutes 45
  libraries 45
  local authorities 45
  Main Statistical Office (GUS) 43–4
  ministries 44
  the press 44–5
  specialised companies 44
  State Agency for Foreign Investment (PAIZ) 43
marketing 137–46
  *introduction* 137–8
  advertising 142–3
  consumer markets 138–9
  distribution 139–41
  fairs/conferences/missions 146
  lack of skills 67
  media 143–5
    press 145
    radio 144–5
    television 143–4
  product positioning 141–2
markets 77–82, 100–2
  capital 77–82
    bonds 80–1
    capital raising 79
    equities 77–9
    investment funds 79
    money matters 81–2

hotel 102
industrial 101–2
office 100–1
retail 101
mass privatisation program (MPP) 20, 34–5, 58, 60–2
media 143–5
  the press 44–5
  press 145
  radio 144–5
  television 143–4
missions, trade 146
money market 55
mortgages 97
municipal bonds 81

Nabarro Nathanson 33–7, 71–5, 105–12, 151–8, 173–6
National Bank of Poland (NBP) *see* Central Bank
National Clearing House (KIR) 54
National Investment Funds (NIF) Law (1993) 61–2
NCM 147–8

office markets 100–1
operational restructuring 67
options for Western business 127–76
  agencies/distributorships/franchises 133–5
  company formation 173–6
    *introduction* 173
    joint stock companies 174–6
    limited liability companies 173–4
  customs and excise 129–32
    administration/procedure 130–1
    duties/international agreements 129–30
    duty free zones/bonded warehouses 131
    excise tax 29–30
    exemptions 131
  intellectual property 151–8
    *introduction* 151
    copyright 151–2
  investment finance 169–72
    bank loans 170
    public debt 170–1
    stock issues 169–70

tax incentives 171–2
investment strategy 163–7
marketing 137–46
  *introduction* 137–8
  advertising 142–3
  consumer markets 138–9
  distribution 139–41
  fairs/conferences/missions 146
  media 143–5
  product positioning 141–2
project finance 159–62
  advantages for borrower/lender 161–2
  borrowers 159–60
  lenders/agents 160
  loan amounts/costs 160
  project characteristics/suitability 160
  security 161
  term 161
trade finance 147–9
  ECGD 148–9
  NCM 147–8
  trade indemnity 148

PAIZ *see* State Agency for Foreign Investment
paper industry 206–7
patents 152–5
  *introduction* 152
  compulsory licensing 154–5
  duration 154
  enforcing rights 155
  international relations 152–3
  inventions created during employment 154
  obtaining rights 153–4
  scope of coverage 153
permanent usufruct 96
permits, strategic area 71–2
PHARE – the new framework 114, 217–19
pharmaceutical industry 207–8
Pilkington 183–5
Polish Brokers Company (PBC) 54
Polish Development Bank (PDB) 81, 161
political transformation 29–32
  back to power 30–2
  the great divide 19–30
ports 122–3
potential, Poland's 19–24

*introduction* 19
establishing a free market economy 20–2
foreign investment 22–4
history 20–1
press, the 44–5, 145
privatisation 34–6, 57–62
  capital 57, 59–60
  case study: Elektrim 179–82
  direct foreign investment 58
  liquidation of SOE 58
  management/employee buy-outs 57–8
  mass privatisation program (MPP) 20, 34–5, 58, 60–2
  restructuring 62
  winding-up 57
product positioning 141–2
profits, repatriation of 51, 74–5
project finance 159–62
  advantages for borrower/lender 161–2
  borrowers 159–60
  lenders/agents 160
  loan amounts/costs 160
  project characteristics/suitability 160
  project finance 161
  security 161
property 33–4, 95–103
  land acquisition permits 73
  real estate 100–3
    hotel markets 102
    industrial markets 101–2
    key considerations 102–3
    office markets 100–1
    retail markets 101
  regulations 95–100
    acquisition/leasing by foreigners 98
    building/development controls 98–9
    expropriation 100
    interests in land 96–7
    land registry 97–8
    restitution 100
    tax 99
  tax 92–3
public debt 170–1

radio 144–5
real estate 100–3
  hotel markets 102
  industrial markets 101–2

key considerations 102–3
office markets 100–1
retail markets 101
redundancy 108–9
  general 108
  procedure 108–9
  severance pay 109
repatriation of profits 51, 74–5
representative offices 75
research and development (R&D) 85
restitution of property 100
restructuring
  and privatisation 62
  state enterprises 63–9
    *introduction* 63
    financial restructuring 65–6
    historical background 63–5
    operational restructuring 67
    the restructuring programme 67–9
retailing sector 101, 209
revaluation of assets 85
roads/ports 122–3
RZB-Austria 25–7, 47–124, 53–5, 147–9, 159–62, 169–72

Saatchi & Saatchi Advertising Poland 137–46
'Scrutiny Act' (1992) 30
sectoral opportunities 197–214
  agriculture 197–8
  automotive 198–9
  brewing 199–200
  chemical 200–1
  coal 201–2
  construction 202–3
  electronics 203–4
  engineering 204–5
  food processing 205–6
  paper 206–7
  pharmaceutical 207–8
  retailing 209
  services 209–10
  shipbuilding/repairs 210–11
  textile/clothing 211–12
  tourism 212–13
  transportation 213–14
semiconductors 157–8
services sector 209–10
severance pay 109

shipbuilding/repairs industry 208
social insurance contributions (ZUS) 92, 112
software 152, 191–3
specialised companies 44
stabilisation projects 221
stamp duty 93
State Agency for Foreign Investment (PAIZ) 43
state enterprises 63–9
  *introduction* 63
  financial restructuring 65–6
  historical background 63–5
  operational issues 67
  the restructuring programme 67–9
stock market
  Stock Exchange, Warsaw 27, 40, 77–8
  stock issues 169–70
strategic area permits 71–2

taxation 89–93
  agricultural 93
  corporate income tax 90
  deferred 86
  excise tax 29–30
  incentives 171–2
  individual income tax 90–1
  property 99
  real property tax 92–3
  social insurance contributions (ZUS) 92
  stamp duty 93
  tax authorities 89–90
  VAT and excise tax 25–6, 91–2
telecommunications 125–6
television 143–4
termination of contracts 106–8
  periods of notice 106
  procedure 107
  restrictions 107
  unlawful upon notice 107
  unlawful without notice 108
  without notice 107–8
textile/clothing sector 134, 209
time off work 111
tourism 212–13
trade finance 147–9
  ECGD 148–9
  NCM 147–8
  trade indemnity 148

trade marks 155–7
    assignment/licensing 156–7
    cancellation 157
    duration 156
    enforcement 157
    international agreements 155
    legislation 155
    protection of foreign marks 155
    registration of 156
    scope of coverage 155–6
trade unions 110
transportation sector 213–14
treasury bills 81

Unicorn Poland 191–3
utilities 123–6
    *introduction* 123
    energy 123–4
    roads/ports 124–5
    telecommunications 125–6

utility models, patents for 158

valuation and accounting 83–7
    accounting policies 84–6
    accounting practices 84
    audit requirements 86–7
    reporting requirements 83–4
VAT and excise tax 25–6, 91–2

Warsaw Stock Exchange 27, 40, 77–8
WIBOR/WIBID (Warsaw Interbank Offer/
    Bid Rates) 82
WIG (stock market index) 78
winding-up privatisation 57
workforce, character of Polish 40–1
working capital 66
working hours/time off 111
World Bank 122, 216

ZUS *see* social insurance contributions